High Flight—Stories of an Air Force Fighter Pilot

High Flight—Stories of an Air Force Fighter Pilot

⚘

Biography of Colonel Lester Romine, USAF Retired

Col. Lester Marlon Romine

With Michele Romine Treacy

High Flight

By John Gillespie Magee Jr.

"Oh I have slipped the surly bonds of Earth, and danced the skies on laughter silvered wings;
Sunward I've climbed and joined the tumbling mirth of sun split clouds-and done a hundred things you have not dreamed of-wheeled and soared and swung high in the sunlight silence.
Hovering there I've chased the shouting wind along and flung my eager craft through footless halls of air
"Up, up the long delirious burning blue, I've topped the wind swept heights with easy grace where never lark or even eagle flew; and, while with silent lifting mind I've trod the high
Untrespassed sanctity of space, put out my hand and touched the face of God.

Copyright © 2016 Col. Lester Marlon Romine
All rights reserved.

ISBN: 1511833440
ISBN 13: 9781511833448

This book is dedicated with love and gratitude to my family and to our honorable and vigilant military men and women who sacrifice so much to protect us and to preserve our freedom here and abroad everyday

Col. Lester Marlon Romine, USAF Ret.
March 2016
Fort Belvoir, Virginia

High Flight
Biography of Lester Marlon Romine

AT THE TIME of this writing, I have lived an amazing life for the past eighty-seven years. I am a cotton farmer's son who dreamed of flying planes as a young man. I am blessed to have made my dreams come true. It has been an honorable adventure of amazing moments…some happy, some sad, some scary, all of them remarkable in their own right and worthy of sharing.

I had a humble start to life on an Alabama farm, which I will detail later. The real adventure started on September 30, 1950, my official entry into the US Air Force.

I was accepted as a cadet into the 13 month pilot training program learning the ropes at air bases in San Angelo Texas and Enid Oklahoma. In October 1951 I graduated from pilot training and received my official commission as an officer.

I reported immediately to San Angelo Texas. The duty here was six weeks of preflight. We marched to all classes, dining, and physical training. The total number in the class was about 120 men. Before the six weeks of preflight ended, we received the scores from the motor tests we had previously taken from Princeton University. About one half of my class was sent home. I recall only one cadet who washed out after we were flying. That cadet was an excellent pilot, but any time the aircraft was rolled or looped, he would vomit. He also was the shortest in height, and he carried about four seat cushions in order to see out of the cockpit.

The basic training was about six months in the T-6 tandem two-seat aircraft. During World War II, the T-6 was the AT-6 advanced trainer for pilot training. We used it as the basic trainer. The instructor flew with us until we soloed in approximately twenty hours. I remember my first flight alone; as the aircraft lifted off, I was past the grass strip and over the wooded area at the auxiliary airfield before I remembered to retract the landing gear and flaps. I was thrilled to be flying for the first time alone and also scared out of my mind. At the time, my only thought was, *How can I get this bird down safely?* And to my surprise, I did! It was the beginning of a twenty-seven-year flying career.

The auxiliary airfield was a grass strip about forty miles from the main base with a stage house where the flight instructors would reside while their students were in their first solo flights. The instructor would be in constant radio contact with his student during these maneuvers. In the T-6, you have a main gear and a tail wheel. This configuration results in a nose high attitude that requires constant zigzagging to clear the area in front of you.

Scary Moments

There were a lot of close calls during training. I recall that another cadet, after successfully completing his solo flight, got a little distracted upon taxiing to the stage house to pick up his instructor. He came very close to crashing into the stage house, the nervous instructor in the stage house shouted loudly over the radio, "Watch out for the stage house," the shaken student jumped onto the brakes, and the screeching aircraft nosed over with the propeller digging into the ground. I think this instructor and student had to get alternate transportation back to our home base on that day.   Lesson learned.

That first-time solo student was not the only one to have a nerve-racking incident. I was attempting a landing in gusty winds at the home base. My instructor was onboard as well. As I rounded out the aircraft, instead of touching down, the aircraft went into a 180-degree right turn, not touching the ground. We ended up off the runway and on the grass. My instructor was concerned that the wing tip may have touched the ground. When we arrived in the parking area, a team of experts examined both wing tips and declared that there was no damage. If the wing tip dragged along the ground, it was an automatic washout or dismissal from the program. My instructor said that the incident was so rapid with the wind rotating the aircraft that he was unable to make any correction.

Tragically we lost two people during basic training. I recall that an instructor and student failed to break out of a downward spin that occurred when the student lost control of the aircraft upon a landing attempt. They tragically crashed in a fruit orchard about six miles east of the base. Fatal accidents like this one made me realize the awesome power and responsibility of flying these expensive and dangerous aircraft. I also mourned the loss of life. It could have been me.

When you graduate from basic training, your instructor determines whether you advance to single- or twin-engine aircraft. My instructor stated that I should attend single-engine advanced fighter training.

My thinking was to serve my required tour of about five years and get out and fly with the commercial airlines. I requested multiengine advanced training. I arrived at Vance Air Force Base in Enid, Oklahoma. The advanced training consisted of two aircraft: the T-28 single engine and the twin-engine B-25 World War II bomber, the one that bombed Japan off an aircraft carrier during the early part of the war. We did not know at this time that over half of my class would be assigned to single-engine fighter interceptors equipped with radar capable of intercepting potential Russian bombers. Our government was considering that Russia might be using the proxy operation in Korea to divert our attention from a full-scale attack.

Our government began a massive expansion program for air defense that included fighter interceptors equipped with radar and joining our air defense with the Canadians. The North American Air Defense Command was established at Colorado Springs, Colorado.

T-28

The T-28 was a tandem single-engine aircraft with a hood in the rear cockpit for instrument flying. The front cockpit pilot would line up the aircraft on the runway and pass control to the rear cockpit pilot. The rear cockpit pilot would check the exact location of the compass needle and push the throttle to full, release the brakes, and roll. He would keep the compass needle at the correct heading by tapping the left and right brakes until the rudders were effective at about seventy knots. Then when they reached the flying speed of eighty knots, the pilot would lift the nose of the aircraft up ten degrees and trim to hold, and the aircraft would fly off the runway. The next step was to retract the landing gear and the flaps. I soloed in the T-28 in about three flights.

One week later, I was in the front cockpit as safety observer and made the takeoff and turn out of traffic climbing to four thousand feet. I adjusted the throttle and pitch control and observed that the pitch control was hung up at two thousand revolutions per minute (RPM). The prop control rod that controls the pitch of the propeller was broken. My heart skipped a beat! Keeping in mind the seriousness of the moment, I recalled all my training and I calmly called the instructor located back on the air base. He advised me not to move any power controls. I said a prayer and I flew a glide pattern as if the engine were not operating with the landing gear and flaps retracted until I was sure of landing on the runway. This was probably the best landing I ever made. I know that God was watching over me that day and for the rest of the my combat missions. A guardian angel sitting in the cockpit with me.

The air force T-28 service was terminated because this was the second incident in about one week. The previous incident was with an instructor and student onboard when the rod snapped at full power and the propeller was wildly spinning and separated from the aircraft engine. They had to dead stick the aircraft beside the runway at the municipal airport with landing gear and flaps retracted. This was known as a belly landing. They did not have enough altitude to glide to the runway.

T-6 And B-25

At this time the faithful T-6 was brought in to fill the gap and provide us with about thirty hours of instrument instruction before advancing to the B-25. We performed air practice in the B-25 and landings at an auxiliary base about seventy-five miles from the main base. A few flights later, my instructor made his exit from the aircraft with me in the left seat and the other cadet as copilot. We flew around the pattern and back to a landing. The aircraft was very easy to fly but extremely noisy inside the cockpit.

Instructor Fun

My instructor was formerly a commercial airline pilot. He was recalled into the air force as a second lieutenant instructor in the B-25. Needless to say, he was an unhappy camper to be teaching cadets. He had four students, and on each flight two cadets would go up with him. I remember one flight when I was waiting my turn for the left seat. The instructor shut down the right engine; the cadet in the left seat was to feather the right engine and trim the aircraft to fly on one engine, but the cadet mistakenly shut down the left engine. The silence was deafening as we realized both engines were not operating.

The unhappy instructor, who we nicknamed Ichabod Crain because of his height and slight build, was immediately flailing around to get control of the aircraft. He successfully started both engines. A great sigh of relief came over the cockpit when we heard those engines fire up. We were at five thousand feet, so we had time to restart. If we were below five thousand feet, we would not shut the engine down. Instead we would place the throttle to idle position and simulate an engine out procedure.

The stage commander would fly with each of his instructor's students in the B-25 to determine if standards were being met. I was scheduled to fly an instrument flight with the commander. An instrument flight test is done to show the commander that a training pilot is knowledgeable and confident in flying by instrument only. The captain lined the aircraft on the center line of the runway and turned the controls over to me. At this point the hood that prevented me from seeing outside was deployed. This exercise simulated flying in bad weather that would limit visibility. I observed the compass needle and advanced the throttles to maximum power, using the brakes to steer until we reached about seventy knots. Then I activated the rudders to steer the aircraft. At about eighty knots, I trimmed the aircraft ten degrees nose high and the aircraft flew right off the runway.

Shortly after becoming airborne, I retracted the landing gear and flaps. I was instructed to tune in the radio frequency for the alternate airfield and perform a radio range orientation and let down to the alternate airfield. The radio range orientation was a bit complicated with Morse code dots and dashes to assist in identifying your location. I performed the radio range orientation and descended to 1500 feet over the radio range station, which was located about seven miles from the alternate airfield runway. Next, I eased the plane down to about 700 feet per minute, with the landing gear and flaps extended and a predetermined heading aligned with the runway and a specific time to be over the runway at 500 feet. I was to tell the commander when we were over the runway. I did and he told me to discard the hood and look outside. We were over the center of the runway. The captain told me this was the best instrument takeoff, range orientation, and let down he had observed.

We did not lose any aircrews during advanced training. I graduated from pilot training on October 27, 1951, and was commissioned as a second lieutenant in the air force.

Fighter Jet Training

I was on vacation in December 1951 to January 1952 with orders to report to Moody AFB in Valdosta, Georgia, to check out in jet fighters. While on vacation, I observed a nighttime air refueling of fighter aircraft flying above my house on a tanker pattern between Birmingham, Alabama, and

Nashville, Tennessee. I wondered how I could ever be able to perform this very complex operation. Details on this unique experience later.

My first flight was in a T-33 tandem jet trainer with an instructor in the backseat. I marveled when I pushed the throttle forward, not seeing a propeller up front that we were moving forward. I soloed in a few flights and flew the F-80 jet fighter during my transition. Then I moved to Tyndall AFB, Florida, to check out and transition in the F-94B. This was a modified T-33 with the radar and the radar operator in the rear cockpit and all the instruments and flight controls removed from the rear cockpit. The engine was the same as the T-33 but with an afterburner installed in the tail for an extra boost of power in combat and the nose of the aircraft extended to house the radar antenna. We practiced landings and air-to-air radar intercepts. I graduated from this course in March, 1952 with my radar observer assigned as my crew member.

We shipped to Elmendorf AFB in Anchorage, Alaska. Our assignment was to the Sixty-Fourth Fighter Interceptor Squadron. As a new second lieutenant, I flew close formation, takeoff, and airborne in the F-94B for approximately one year, and then I became a flight leader. The flight leader is a leader of two to four aircraft in formation for the squadron. I work with the commander and communicate the orders to our squadron pilots. We practiced firing our machine guns on a towed target. We would line up the tow aircraft, an F-94B, on the runway, and the armament crew would attach the one-thousand-foot cable to the underside fuselage of the tow aircraft. The target was a small mesh nylon target, thirty feet long and about twelve feet wide. The target was placed flat on the runway and the tow cable attached in the middle of a twelve-foot-long, two-inch diameter iron bar that became the leading edge of the target. The tow aircraft would reach takeoff speed before the target would rotate upright. And after becoming airborne, the aircraft would fly at a speed of 175 knots during the mission. We would dip our machine gun bullets in different colored paint so that each firing aircraft could determine who hit the target.

We returned the target to the active runway and released it on the grass next to the runway. The armament crew would pick it up and deliver it to our location for scoring. Our mission here was air defense, with a secondary mission of close air support for ground troops. The secondary mission would occur only if we were under attack and the regular fighter bomber close air support aircraft were not present. I was honored to be the flight leader for this and many other squadrons, I always took my role model responsibilities seriously in an effort to teach the young ones the ropes.

Survival Of The Fittest

I was assigned as the forward air controller for an exercise with the army out in the snow for three days. Our meals were the famous "C" rations, tasty dried or canned meals like beef or spaghetti with meatballs and some dry meals that did not taste very good. I performed my mission in a tracked vehicle equipped with a UHF radio and driver. The army would tell me where the target they wanted to eliminate was located and the run-in heading for the delivery of the weapon, and I would relay this information to the airborne fighter. The run in heading intelligence was crucial to ensure that we did not bomb "friendlies."

When on five-minute alert, we were able to be airborne, wearing all our arctic survival gear, in about three minutes. This layered gear was heavy! We wore this equipment for the entire twenty-four hours we were on alert and this included sleeping. The temperature varied at the time we were there. During the summer, the average temperature was eighty degrees in Anchorage. In winter, the temperature was near zero most of the time, and we had some thirty below days on a couple of occasions during my two-year tour. When the air defense radar scrambled us for a target, we were required to be airborne in five minutes. The radar site we worked with was located just off the end of our runway on an island in Cook Inlet. Most of our intercepts were small aircraft piloted by bush pilots. With our speeds it was difficult to slow down and stay with the target. We would perform "S" turns if the controller requested a tail number of the aircraft.

We rotated aircraft and crews with maintenance personnel to King Salmon Airfield, located about eighty miles southeast of Nome, Alaska. We placed two aircraft on five-minute alert to cover the western border of Alaska, the Gulf, and the islands to the south. A catholic priest who had been in the wilds of Alaska for most of his life approached me at King Salmon. He requested I get him a flight back to Anchorage on one of our supply transports. I did this, and later at Anchorage he found me again and requested I get him a flight in a jet to Fairbanks. My ops officer approved, and we launched with four aircraft on a navigation and close formation training flight with the priest in my backseat, heading northwest until we crossed the Arctic Circle, and then fly a heading back southeast to Ladd Air Force Base located in Fairbanks. He was thrilled for an opportunity to fly across the Arctic Circle, since he had never been that far north during his tour and I assume he was in the process of retiring back to the States.

Tough Training
About one-third of our pilots in the Fifty-Seventh Fighter Group were new second lieutenants, recently graduated from pilot training. A significant number of our losses were experienced crew. We practiced air combat maneuvers, dogfights, and on one occasion one of our pilots traveling at a very high speed lost the right wing when it separated from the fuselage. The speed and g-forces created a tense moment, but with full aileron and rudder, the pilot was in level flight long enough to pull the ejection handle before he lost control of the aircraft. Unfortunately, the pilot was severely injured during the ejection from the aircraft; both kneecaps were severed from the thigh muscle and were hanging when he was picked up from a lake in shallow water. The ejection seat has a rocket attached and the seat travels up a track attached to the back side

of the seat. This pilot was over six feet tall and measured over fifty-eight inches from hip to knee. The forward wind screen on his aircraft severed his kneecaps as the seat traveled up and out of the aircraft. After this event, any pilot who measured over fifty-eight inches from hip to knee was not permitted to fly in fighters. Another pilot was performing this same maneuver, and when he disengaged from this activity, he was too close to the ground and had to pull heavy g-forces to avoid flying into the ground, and the aircraft went into a high-speed stall, flipped over on its back, and crashed inverted into the trees. He did not survive. Sadly, he did not get to see his new child, as his wife was due to give birth at the time of the accident.

During my two-year tour my squadron lost two pilots. The radar operator on one of the aircraft survived with injuries. During World War II, this radar operator was a navigator and had to bailout of a C-46 in China. He then became a pilot and was flying a P-51 fighter on takeoff when the engine quit and he had to eject from that aircraft as well. This accident in Alaska was his third with flash burns and bone fractures, and in his hospital bed, he stated to me that this was his last flying assignment.

The second pilot was flying alone. The Sixty-Fifth Squadron lost three crew members during this period, and the Sixty-Sixth Squadron lost about eighteen. The Sixty-Sixth replaced at least three commanders, and the Alaskan Air Command retired one general officer. Some of those lost were in the soft mud in Cook Inlet and some were above the ninety-five-hundred-foot level on the mountains. The soft mud covers debris at the impact point, and the snow never melts higher than 9500 feet; the avalanche of snow covers the impact area. About six aircrew remains were never found.

Unidentified Flying Object

At this point, I will share an experience of a UFO event reported to air defense radar from the cockpit of a commercial airliner in route from

Fairbanks to Anchorage. The two pilots reported to the air defense radar what they considered to be a UFO about six miles north of our location. This was a nighttime sighting. The radar controller requested that I launch one aircraft and investigate. I launched from runway 26 and made a right turn over the radar site on the island below my position. As I turned north and changed my radio to the radar frequency, they immediately advised me that the object had vanished. They stated that the object could accelerate from zero to sixteen hundred miles per hour as rapidly as you could blink your eye. The object could make a ninety-degree angle turn without losing any airspeed. This was a solid object before radar could pick it up, and then on the next radar sweep, it was not solid anymore, and at this point you could not see it visually. My radar operator and I knew this was one of those unexplainable events, and it was a bit shocking. I was told to return to the base. In my opinion, I had witnessed a supernatural event, and I believe it was a UFO.

Brrrr!

During our tour each aircrew, both the pilot and radar operator, was required to attend the arctic survival training course. We scheduled our trip in April, hoping for good, warm weather. When we departed Anchorage on the train, the temperature was thirty below zero, and when we arrived in Fairbanks, the temperature was fifty-four below zero. That was cold! The ice fog was heavy. We had walkers to steer us through the heavy ice fog by bus to our quarters. The first two days, we were in ground school, and we could attend all activities by passing through below-ground tunnels. After the two days in classroom briefings, we went out into the field. We experienced a heat wave as the temperature went from fifty-four below to thirty below. The rules were if the temperature was more than thirty below zero on the first night, we would go back into base quarters. No such luck for us, as we were required to stay out a second night.

The Can Of Beans Incident

I recall a couple of funny incidents where a number of people were leaning over the fire with their hands outstretched. Someone had placed a can of beans in the fire to warm them before eating, and they failed to punch holes in the can top, and it blew up, and everyone had to wipe beans off their eyebrows!

The second incident was an army major on the first night who rotated his layered sleeping bag over his face and experienced claustrophobia and had to tear the bag to get out. The second night he just pulled or zipped the bag up to his chest area and slept sitting up, leaning against a row of boxes. But it was not all fun and games, as I remember getting out of my sleeping bag and chopping wood in the dark of night just to stay warm.

Medical Emergency Flight

One night when I was on alert, I received an emergency phone call to transport urgently needed medication from Anchorage to a hospital in Fairbanks. For something like this to occur, we knew a very high-level governmental official or general officer had to be seriously ill. This medication was flown from Seattle to Anchorage by commercial aircraft and by speeding car to our aircraft. I quickly scrambled my crew and hopped in the plane. The order was for us to travel to Ladd AFB in Fairbanks as fast as we could go, and someone would meet us at the aircraft and transport the medication to the local hospital. We used full throttle and afterburner as needed to maintain a speed near maximum for the aircraft. We made the 280-mile trip in less than forty minutes, flying low level in the valley along the east side of the twenty-thousand-foot Mount McKinley on the north course to Fairbanks. This was the time of the year in Alaska when it was day light at 3:00 a.m. and visibility was good. We had twilight conditions for about three hours over the midnight period. I was never told for whom the medication was intended; I did know that many of our congressmen and senior generals hunted in Alaska.

High Flight—Stories of an Air Force Fighter Pilot

The Lockheed Company manufactured the three aircraft during this period. They were all modifications of the basic T-33 airframe. The maximum airspeed for all three was 505 knots (F-80, T-33, F-94B). Each of these aircraft was equipped with four fifty-caliber caliber machine guns.

When I was leaving Alaska in 1954, the Sixty-Fifth Squadron was equipped with the F-89C with four twenty-millimeter guns. On one incident, an F-89C aircraft from the Sixty-Fifth Squadron launched and climbed on a north heading to about twenty thousand feet and made a left turn at Mount McKinley. It suddenly went nose down and crashed into the ground at a very high rate of speed. There were no communications from the crew. No one survived. The investigation was not complete when I departed Alaska. The initial assumption was toxic fumes or oxygen problems in the cockpit. My squadron was receiving the F-89D equipped with 2.75-inch airborne folding fin rockets, with fifty-two in each wing pod. My tour in Alaska was complete, and I did not fly the F-89D.

My new assignment was the Ninety-Sixth Fighter Interceptor Squadron (FIS) located at New Castle County Airport, Delaware. The F-94C was a much larger aircraft with a powerful J-47 engine (same engine as the B-47 six-jet-engine bomber) with an afterburner and a radar operator in the backseat. This aircraft at its maximum speed was just below supersonic. This was a different aircraft than the previous ones and was given this designation for congressional funding accountability only.

The mission here was a continuation of air defense off the east coast of the United States. Our nation designated an air defense zone out to about one hundred miles over the Atlantic Ocean. All aircraft entering the zone from overseas locations were required to enter the zone within close tolerance of speed, heading, and certain turns before continuing on course to their destination in the United States.

Yet Another Unidentified Flying Object

On one occasion, I was directed to this location on a night scramble to intercept an unidentified target. When I was close enough to identify the target as one of ours, the ground controller requested that I follow this aircraft to New York City. The controller indicated that this aircrew was in continuous violation of our rules and for me to move in close enough to the tail of the aircraft in the lights over New York City and direct my radar operator to shine his flashlight on the tail number of the aircraft and for me to forward it to him. They were in the process of filing a violation on this airline and its crew.

As I mentioned earlier, the F-94C aircraft was subsonic, and we would go up to forty thousand feet and point the nose of the aircraft almost straight down with full throttle until the wings would rock right and left, and then the nose of the aircraft would attempt to tuck under. At this point I would immediately throttle to idle and speed brakes down. If you proceed, the aircraft will flip end over end and would probably disintegrate as it was trying to penetrate the supersonic zone.

We deployed to Yuma, Arizona, for thirty days each year to fire rockets at airborne towed targets. Colonel Ben King, our group commander, requested the All American Engineering firm located on the air base to design and install an airborne target system on one of our T-33 aircraft. They fabricated a spool with a one-thousand-foot cable. The target was in the shape of a bomb, about four feet long and two feet in diameter with fins on the rear. The cable was connected to a steel plate on the nose of the target. This plate gave the firing fighter radar operator two distinct radar blips at a ninety-degree angle; the tow aircraft up front and the target one thousand feet behind. When this system was ready for test, Colonel King requested that I fly the T-33 and he would ride in the backseat and operate the electrical switches that controlled the target system. We traveled out over the Atlantic Ocean. We made several successful deployments, and then reeled the target into the storage basket. This became the target system we used for all rocket practice. The F-94C could carry forty-eight 2.75-inch folding fin rockets. For practice, we would load only six rockets.

At Yuma, I met Lt. Col. Daniel James, the commander of another squadron assigned to our wing. I also met Major Jabara. He was assigned to the headquarters at Yuma. Colonel James later became the first African American four star general. Major Jabara was killed in a head-on car accident in Florida a few years later. He survived fifteen MIG air kills to his credit during the Korean War; at the time that was the highest number of kills for any one of our pilots during the Korean War. Tragically an automobile accident took his life.

One incident at Yuma that I remember was an aircrew that fired six rockets at a tow aircraft with two pilots onboard. Two rockets went over the aircraft, two went under, and two passed in front of the tow aircraft. These rockets were with practice warheads, but if one had penetrated the canopy of the tow aircraft, it would have been very serious. The procedure was to make a ninety-degree angle pass to the tow aircraft. From this position it was very easy to see two distinct targets on the radar of the firing aircraft, and you were supposed to lock on the target behind the tow airplane. If the firing aircraft pilot looked out to the point where the nose of his aircraft was aimed far ahead of the tow aircraft, then his radar operator was mistakenly locked on to the tow aircraft and not the target behind. Each pilot in the squadron was subject to being a tow pilot in the T-33.

The aircraft has forty-eight rockets, with twenty-four in a ring around the radar antenna up front, and twelve each in a pod on the left and the right wings. There were no records that the full load of forty-eight rockets had ever been fired at once. I was sent to Florida to use the offshore range and fire the full load into the water. There were no problems with the rockets around the nose of the aircraft, but the wing pods caused the skin to buckle where the pod was anchored into the wing. Some repairs were required for the entire fleet to secure the wing pods.

On another mission at Eglin AFB, Florida, I was the number four pilot in a flight of four aircraft with a mission to shoot down a drone B-17 four-engine World War II bomber with filming to be shown on the Dave Garroway television show the next day. The number one fighter was an F-89D with 104 combat rockets all fired at once. The B-17 was smashed into many pieces. I could see about a twelve-foot section of the B-17 wing with an engine in the middle of it and the propeller ceasing its rotation. The number two F-89D fired his 104 rockets into the many broken pieces, and by this time the junk was far down below and number three and I, in the number four position, were not able to fire. The bad news was that the camera onboard the four-engine transport aircraft malfunctioned, and we were not able to see ourselves on television the next day. But my five minutes of fame soon followed.

Hollywood, Here I Come!

On another assignment I flew with two aircraft to Eglin AFB, Florida, on a unique mission. We were to fly five missions in the movie, *Toward the Unknown*. The movie was made in 1956. This movie was a test pilot story with Lloyd Nolan, William Holden, and Virginia Leith as the principal actors. Most of the movie was made at the Edwards AFB test facility in California, including flying missions and some filming in the Officers Club. The flight operations were shifted to Eglin AFB in Florida to get some camera shots with large thunderhead clouds in the background. These thunderheads were not available over the desert in California. The movie crew consisted of the famous stunt pilot, Paul Manse. Manse had his own air force of World War II aircraft. He crashed landed a B-17 bomber in the movie, *Twelve O'clock High*. Hiring a copilot cost more money than he wanted to pay, and he flew the B-17 mission alone.

He used the World War II B-25 bomber as the camera aircraft for this movie. Paul was doing very well, as I was told that he lived on a one-hundred-foot yacht off the coast of California. One night, a generous Paul loaned me and another pilot his 1955 specially designed auto with electrical switches from bumper to bumper. At this time, this was probably the only car with this advanced capability, and we had it as our very own for the night. Oh what fun we had with that fancy car! We cruised around town like we owned the place. A memorable time for sure for this humble cotton farmer's son. We managed to return it to him with no damage. Additional aircraft came from Edwards AFB for more filming. One of them was the XB-51. This was an underpowered three-engine bomber aircraft that never went into production. Instead, the air force bought the British Canbera twin-engine bomber. When the last XB-51 in the inventory was in route from Edwards AFB, it crashed on takeoff at El Paso, Texas, killing the pilot and crew chief. It was a very hot day, and the elevation of the runway at El Paso was about forty-five hundred feet. The thin air and heat were bad news for an underpowered aircraft.

The weather did not cooperate in Florida. A stationary front was in the area, and after about four days, we were ordered to launch. The cloud ceiling was six hundred feet overcast, and we were on top of everything at about four thousand feet with no desired thunderheads in view. A sub-plot of the movie centered on the first drag chutes that were installed for braking purposes on the aircraft to reduce the very expensive brake replacement. It entered in the minds of some experts that this could be used as an airborne tactic when an enemy fighter was in firing position directly behind you. The pilot under attack could deploy his drag chute, and the very rapid deceleration of his aircraft would cause the enemy to fly past him, and then he would release his drag chute, and he would be in a perfect position to shoot the enemy aircraft down in front of him. Great concept!

During this experimental test with the F-94C at Edwards AFB test facility in California, the drag chute failed to release. An attempt was made to use full throttle with afterburner to burn the drag chute off, and it failed. With a fully deployed drag chute, the aircraft nose was pointing almost straight down. At this point, the test pilot had to make a decision to either bail out or attempt a very dangerous landing. The major decided on a landing attempt. He made the descent at a very steep angle and had to quickly round out just before the aircraft touched the ground. The aircraft hit the ground very hard and was heavily damaged. The pilot was able to exit the wreck, and as he was running out on the wing, the fuel ignited and he was seriously burned on the thigh of his leg. The fire vehicles arrived and extinguished the fire. This unique test event was used as the theme of the movie.

This same test pilot was with us at Eglin, and on off days, when we were water skiing, he would drive the boat to avoid stress on his leg. The story line for the movie centered on Lloyd Nolan, whose character was the brigadier general and base commander of the test facility. Also in the movie was William Holden, who played former Korean War prisoner, Major Lincoln Bonds, who was given a new lease on life by the general (Lloyd Nolan).

I was the stunt pilot in one particular flight scene in the movie where the general (Lloyd Nolan) moved into position and placed his wing tip fuel tank into the drag chute of Major Lincoln Bonds. I flew the plane for Lloyd Nolan's character. My friend Curt Thor flew the plane for William Holden. This maneuver collapsed the drag chute and placed both planes into close formation. They then flew back to the base together and landed both aircraft in close formation at touchdown. In the movie we placed a strong test strip around the outer rim of the drag chute to prevent it from deploying fully as it was used on the runway for braking. With this configuration we could launch and land with it deployed. I must admit I had a ball working on this movie, what a great experience! And years later, I watched the movie with family – what fun memories.

I served three and a half memorable years at New Castle County Joint Commercial/Air Force Base, and during this time I was offered and accepted a regular commission. At this time the air force was operating with two-thirds of the officers as reservists and one-third as regular commissioned officers. The order was reversed to assure a trained force to be available for the long, drawn-out Cold War that followed. If there was any reduction in the force, the reserves were the first to be released. The regular commission gave me security for a long career in the air force.

Supersonic

I was promoted to captain and assigned to McGuire AFB in New Jersey to fly the F-102 air defense delta wing fighter interceptor. This was my first supersonic aircraft with speeds of 930 miles per hour. Keep in mind that Mach one is 760 miles per hour. I was responsible for air defense here, and with only one crew member in the aircraft, I was required to operate my own radar. The control stick at the top was shaped like a U, and with the left handle unlocked, it became the radar hand control to move the antenna to search for a target.

During this time, I met a former Tuskegee Airmen pilot, Lt. Col. Woodrow Wilson Crockett, who served in the headquarters of the New York Air Defense Sector. We had a tour of the very large computerized blockhouse that was built to withstand a nuclear blast, called the SAGE building, located at McGuire. SAGE stands for Semiautomatic Ground Environment. The main door to this amazing building was at least ten feet thick! All New York air defense radars up and down the coast feed into this computerized blockhouse, and the radar controllers direct us to our targets.

This F-102 Interceptor was capable of altitudes over fifty thousand feet. We had to wear a pressure suit on at least one orientation flight above fifty thousand feet. The air pressure was so thin that if you lost the aircraft cabin pressure at fifty thousand or above and did not have a pressure suit, your blood would bubble out of suspension. The tactics of our potential enemy changed, and we were not required to wear a pressure suit when on alert duty. At the time, these pressure suits were considered to be the latest high technology to protect pilots at high altitudes. This pressure suit was a sign of the uncertain geo-political climate at the time. I remember thinking it was a lot like wearing a space suit!

I had an interesting experience on this one orientation flight above fifty thousand feet over the Atlantic Ocean. Heading east you could see the curvature of the Earth as the smoke from a ship heading west could be observed before the ship came into view. The ship appeared to be moving uphill toward me. What an amazing sight to behold.

In 1959 the entire F-102 aircraft fleet had a low in commission rate, which meant that each squadron did not have all the necessary aircraft replacement parts to ensure combat readiness. The air force chief of staff ordered our squadron to deploy to Panama City, Florida, and with all personnel positions filled and all the parts for the aircraft for a sixty-day buildup and thirty-day simulated combat. The aircraft performed extremely well. After a lock on to a target drone, I put the arm switch on and engaged the autopilot. Similar to when using the cruise control in a car, I could place my feet on the floor and fold my arms. The aircraft would fire automatically. We could perform hands-off autopilot, connected with the instrument landing system (ILS) final approach to the runway, disengage, and land the aircraft. This ninety-day test confirmed that the aircraft would perform as designed with a generous supply of replacement parts available at each squadron location and all authorized personnel positions filled to ensure that the squadron was combat ready at a moment's notice. The supply chain needed some improvement in speed of moving parts to the squadron location.

I served in New Jersey for one year, and the squadron was moved to England AFB in Alexandria, Louisiana, on very short notice. What prompted this move was a light aircraft that flew from Havana, Cuba to the commercial airport in New Orleans. No one knew he was coming until he landed. Needless to say this created quite a bit of anxiety, since Russia and Cuba were very close allies. Most of our air defense capability was directed over Canada and the northern routes. We moved our squadron to England AFB, Louisiana, and radar assets to cover the southern routes. I was on air defense duty here for one year.

Jetting On The Jet Stream

I was sent to California to ferry an F-102 from the modification center to England AFB in Louisiana. Normally we would stop in Denver, Colorado, to refuel. This trip was unique because the jet stream was usually from twenty-eight thousand to thirty-eight thousand feet, and very rarely was it on a straight course to your destination. This jet stream was at forty-five thousand feet on a straight course to southern Georgia. Conveniently this jet stream was moving directly over my home base, west to east at a speed of 210 miles per hour. My F-102 had a true air speed of 530 miles per hour at this altitude. When you add the two figures together, I was flying over the ground at a speed of 740 miles per hour. The ground traffic controllers were excited and telling me if I could add another twenty knots that I would be traveling over the ground at supersonic speed. I will remember this near supersonic flight for the rest of my life. There are a few moments in life when I am completely speechless and in awe of the amazing power of our planet. I flew nonstop from California to my home base in Alexandria, Louisiana, with plenty of reserve fuel.

During the summer of 1960, ten of the aircraft and crews were relocated to Iceland. We flew a number of our F-102 aircraft to the National Guard in Houston, Texas. On one of my trips to Houston, my operations officer directed me to brief the National Guard pilots on the technical order capabilities of the F-102. I cycled through the order with about twenty National Guard pilots during a four-hour period. Our future president George W. Bush was not present, but he did later fly as a pilot in the F-102.

Britain

At this time I was assigned to Sculthorpe Air Base, United Kingdom, as a victor alert duty officer. This position was to increase the number of personnel in the nuclear launch cycle of the Forty-Seventh Bomb Wing flying the B-66 light bomber with targets in Eastern Europe. This was my first overseas trip, and I was thrilled to live in a foreign country. I had this duty for two years armed with a .45 caliber pistol.

I can recall one incident when I was the duty officer on the alert pad about twenty yards from an aircraft loaded with nuclear weapons. One night after going on duty at 8:00 p.m., I heard a pop. It was one of the air police guards who had aimed his rifle at the vertical tail of one of the nuclear-loaded aircraft and shot a hole in it. He just lost control, and this was considered a nuclear mishap known as a broken arrow. This kind of action got the attention up the chain of command to the Pentagon. Mass confusion ensued until we had a replacement aircraft loaded and on alert.

At this location I was flying the T-33 jet at the end of the week to maintain proficiency. Two pilots were given an aircraft on Friday, with approval to fly to any friendly country in Europe and return on Sunday night with a minimum of eight hours on the aircraft. Each pilot logged pilot time in the front cockpit and copilot time in the rear cockpit.

On one of these flights to Madrid, Spain, we landed in France on the way back to England to refuel and had to rush to get airborne before a vicious thunderstorm crossed over the airfield. Amid looming clouds and crashing thunder, We rushed our takeoff because I was scheduled to be the duty officer on the alert pad at 8:00 p.m. that evening. The T-33 does not have radar, so we requested the French radar controllers to provide us a vector around the storm. They ran us right through the middle of the storm. No wonder the French have such a bad reputation! Fear briefly overcame me then I exhaled and took control. I was pilot in the front cockpit and flying the aircraft. The air speed indicator was rotating from 0 to 275 miles per hour, and ice formed all over the canopy and the wings. We had to fly on instruments, and you had to avoid the air speed indicator and bring in to your view all instruments that have any bearing with the attitude or position of the aircraft in relation to the ground. We could not see out. The aircraft was giving us a very violent ride. This was the only thunderstorm that I flew through the area of violent up and down drafts in the center of the storm during my entire career. This was a short trip to England, and we had plenty of fuel. We were fortunate as we let down over the English Channel that the freezing level was about twelve thousand feet, the ice melted and slid off the wings and canopy, and we were able to make a safe landing. If the freezing level that day had been at the surface of the earth, the ice would not melt off the canopy and wings; then we would have to bail out. You cannot land if you cannot see the runway.

The nuclear bomb wing was retired and the aircraft flown to Tucson for storage. In 1962, most of the personnel who had been in fighters before were transferred to France to man the F-84F fighter bombers that the National Guard deployed to France during the Berlin Crisis in 1961. The National Guard personnel were sent home.

Bonjour, France

The four aircraft squadrons were placed under the 366th Tactical Fighter Wing headquarters. They were the 389th, 390th, 391th, and 480th Squadrons. I was assigned to the 389th Squadron in Chaumont, France. The wing headquarters also was located here at Chaumont. It is here that I met two men who would become my best friends, Drury Callahan and Roger Schmitt. Bonded together by our training and in combat, our friendships have endured the test of time. I am grateful for our time together. At Chaumont, we deployed in small numbers for about three weeks of simulated combat, weapons delivery, and gunnery training to Tripoli, Libya. I remember flying a navigation training flight over the desert with no roads or other navigation points, only miles and miles of sand. It was definitely a harrowing challenge to navigate and not get lost over the vast desert and sand with no visible landmarks in the Middle East. We used only time and distance and compass heading while flying on a box pattern to arrive back at the base. When we finished our three weeks of training, a transport aircraft brought us home and another group made the journey. We practiced all combat training except midair refueling.

After one year in France, I received a telegram with official orders to arrive later to report back to the United States. The telegram stated that this was a secret assignment. Within about two weeks of this notification, the wing headquarters received orders for the entire wing to deploy back to Holloman AFB in New Mexico. My wing commander cancelled my previous order and stated that I would return to the United States with the fighter wing. I have often wondered if the secret assignment was a position with the reconnaissance program of the U-2 or Blackbird units.

At the time of the orders to return to the United States, we had not performed any midair refueling practice, even though the aircraft were equipped for this activity. When we deployed to the United States, we flew a distance of about seven hundred miles on each leg, and then we would stop and refuel. Our journey was from France to Scotland, Iceland, Greenland, Goose Bay Labrador, McGuire AFB New Jersey, Little Rock, Arkansas, and then a final stop at Holloman AFB. Quite a long journey!

When I made my aircraft start in France, I experienced a false start with much smoke pouring out of the tailpipe and the air scoop up front. This happened occasionally, but this time, a major general, not knowing that my aircraft was the next to start, was leaning against the nose of my aircraft, and he quickly ran a race to get clear. I cycled the engine to clear out raw fuel in the tailpipe to prevent an explosion for the next start attempt. The next start was normal; however this false start may have signaled a potential emergency that occurred later. We landed in Scotland and remained overnight with our entire fleet of eighty aircraft. Our families were there with us because their transport aircraft had an engine problem and were stranded there overnight. We departed the next day in flights of four aircraft in formation with four-minute spacing between flights. The airborne command post was with us in a large C135 aircraft as we were flying over the water.

This command post aircraft was equipped with long-range communication and a senior officer onboard. He had the capability to speak to any navy rescue ships or aircraft underneath our route. Only two aircraft had difficulties for the entire trip. The first was an aircraft that landed in the Shetland Islands near the coast of England with an escort for safety. A short time later, I had a generator failure about three hundred miles before landing in Iceland. My heart sank as I could hear the melted wiring from the generator going through the compressor blades in the engine. Not a good sound! I was very fortunate that not one of the compressor blades broke free. Had one of the blades broke free, it would be like knocking over pins at the bowling alley. It would have destroyed the engine. Yet another example of my guardian angel looking out for me.

With a generator failure, you have about twenty minutes of battery power available; at this point you lose the radio, speed brakes, and landing gear activation. I reported this to my lead and knew that if we penetrated the clouds I could see in the distance, my radio would be inoperative and the speed brakes would not deploy. I requested that he not use speed brakes in the descent, but as we entered the clouds about twenty minutes later, he did deploy the speed brakes, and suddenly I was all alone in the clouds. I had to orient myself on instruments and turn forty-five degrees to the right (I was on the right wing) and travel about two minutes for safety spacing from my flight and then back to the original heading to Iceland. When I was clear of the clouds and flying parallel to the Icelandic Ice Cap, I could see the western end of Iceland about one hundred miles ahead. My landing airport was at the western end of the island. A wave of relief came over me as I made my descent into the airport.

When we fly long flights over water, we have to wear a waterproof suit that fits firm around the wrists, ankles, and neck. When I tested mine before launch, it leaked, and there had been no spare available. If I was required to eject into the cold, icy waters, chances for survival were not good. I steered to the western tip of Iceland and then over the air base. I could see the aircraft that landed before me on the ramp. With my radio inoperative, I flew about one hundred feet above the runway, rocking my wings to signal to the tower controllers that I could not communicate with them. The controllers in the tower cleared all traffic away until I was safely wheels down on the runway. With no electrical power or hydraulics, I had to place the landing gear handle in the down position and violently rock the wings of the aircraft in order for the landing gear to firmly lock in the down position. Electrical power was not available, and without landing flaps, the nose of the aircraft was very high, and this condition required an increase in air speed. I landed safely but could not continue until a new generator was installed five days later.

At this time, the airborne command post launched with the two aircraft from the Shetland Islands and called to me to be airborne at thirty thousand feet at a specific time to join with them. I was able to do this with engine chugs as I advanced the throttle past 80 percent power. The engine ran smoothly at all other power settings, and we flew on to Greenland. I requested the maintenance tech climb into the air scoop and perform an engine compressor blade inspection. He did so and found nicks from the melted generator wiring on most of the compressor blades. The generator on this aircraft was located in the center of the forward end of the engine. Not a very good location if the generator disintegrates during failure with the pieces of junk passing to the rear into the engine compressor blades. I requested an engine change, and they did so overnight and test flew the aircraft. It was ready to go when I arrived the next morning. The airborne command post was with us until we were over land at Goose Bay, Labrador. At this point our three aircraft flew on to New Mexico together.

When we arrived in New Mexico in 1963, the Cuban Missile Crisis was being negotiated with the Russian government. We were assigned targets in and around Havana. Had we been ordered to execute the mission, we were to deploy to Tampa, Florida. We would launch and climb to thirty thousand feet and fly to Key West, and then with a steep descent, fly under radar coverage very low over the water to the assigned target. This issue was resolved with no combat.

Saudi Arabia

In October 1963, my next orders were to travel to Saudi Arabia for a two-month temporary deployment. I traveled by commercial aircraft from New Mexico to New York. While in New York, the aircraft on the run-up pad experienced a locked brake. We were delayed for about two hours and then loaded on a replacement aircraft. I missed my flight connection at Athens, Greece to Saudi Arabia, I remained overnight at Athens, and the next day was on an Ethiopian airline to Cairo. This was where things got dicey. I was in the Cairo Airport for five hours, and the flight to Saudi Arabia was on a Russian-built Czech Airline TU-104. This was a unique experience, as the Czech flight attendant insisted on providing me with propaganda magazines. While on the ground, the crew taxied too fast and the baggage in the overhead bins fell during turns. My seat was next to where the left engine was anchored in the aircraft fuselage. It was very noisy. This was a two-engine aircraft. I was grateful when we landed safely in Saudi Arabia.

It was quite an unusual experience to travel through Cairo, Egypt while knowing our mission was to prevent the political uprising by armed thugs along the border of Saudi Arabia directed by Nasser, the leader of Egypt at that time, with Russian assistance. The temperature in Saudi Arabia was 120 degrees during most of my time there. We had a vehicle for our use, and we used it to get to the Arabian American oil company complex about two miles away. This was a secure and gated community where all the Americans who worked in the oil industry lived with their families. If you need American food or products, it was there. The restaurant was excellent. We ate all our meals there.

We had three F-100 aircraft and two KB-50 Tankers. The F-100 aircraft were located at Jeddah on the Red Sea. I made a visit on a C-130 at five hundred feet above the sand to Jeddah about six hundred miles across nothing but sand with one oasis spring-fed watering location approximately in the center of Saudi Arabia. The many animals that we could see in the area would take turns at the watering location. This included donkeys, camels, sheep, and goats.

I also had a six-hour flight in the four-propeller engine KB-50 tanker as I observed the refueling operation. The tankers were with us near Riyadh at the Dhahran air base on the eastern coast of Saudi Arabia. From the Jeddah location, the F-100 aircraft could stay airborne many hours with tanker refueling. They would fly along the Yemen border at four thousand feet altitude with no weapons deployed. This signaled to those below that the United States was holding hands with Saudi Arabia. There were C-130 courier flights to many locations in Saudi Arabia and other countries in the area. I used this transportation for a weekend trip to Beirut, Lebanon and then to Aden on the southern coast of Yemen to deliver a passenger and from Aden back to our air base near Riyadh. In 1963, Beirut, Lebanon, was a beautiful coastal city known as "Little Paris of the East." We resided in a hotel that was located in a choice location along the beach of the Mediterranean Sea.

During my duty in Saudi Arabia, President Kennedy was shot in Dallas, Texas, that fateful November day. We were awakened at 1:00 a.m. in case there might be more tragic events to follow, not knowing if it was a terrorist attack. We were up for two hours until it was determined that this was not the case. There was not a lot of news coverage of the presidential assassination in Saudi Arabia; however, we received detailed briefings through military communication channels.

Alamogordo, New Mexico

I returned to New Mexico in December 1963. In late summer 1964, the Wing was returning the F-84F to the National Guard, and we were ferrying new F-4C aircraft from the factory in Saint Louis, Missouri. The air refueling operation was very easy in both the F-84F and the F-4C Phantom II. It was just a matter of good formation, and we had many hours at this point. The boom operator in the tanker had very good control of the boom. He could extend or retract and move it right or left. As you moved into position, the boom operator directed you to within feet of the connection by radio. As you look forward, you could see amber, red, and green lights on the forward undersection of the tanker fuselage. When you were at the proper elevation angle to observe the green light, you were in the correct elevation position for refueling. At night, this maneuver was just like pulling your car into a lighted service station and shouting, "Fill her up with high test!"

High Flight—Stories of an Air Force Fighter Pilot

At this point, your refueling receptacle was open, and the boom operator spoke to you to hold everything and stay in this formation position. Almost immediately you could feel the boom from a slight rotation of your aircraft when it connected into your receptacle. As you observed the fuel instrument in your cockpit rapidly moving upward, within minutes you had about two thousand pounds of fuel uploaded. The F-84F receptacle was in the left wing near the fuselage, and the boom would pass by near the left side of my cockpit. The receptacle on the F-4C was located behind the rear copilot cockpit, and this required the boom to pass right over my front cockpit position. We performed refueling practice at night also and on some occasions with all the tanker lights turned off, which of course was more interesting and challenging.

In December 1964, I had recently been promoted to major and assigned as chief of the Wing Command Post with three duty officers and twenty enlisted airmen for around-the-clock operation. I traveled to Tucson with other headquarters personnel to attend the ground school and airborne program on learning to fly in the F-4C Phantom II. The third flight in the F-4C was at Mach 2, which is over sixteen hundred miles per hour, with an instructor onboard. We finished the course with our copilot as a crew. When the air force purchased the F-4C, it was equipped in the rear cockpit with the radar set and controls, a full instrument panel, throttles and stick control. The copilot in the rear cockpit operated the radar and could fly the airplane on instruments if necessary.

During nighttime combat when changing the weapon switches in the front cockpit, the copilot would fly the airplane. If we were performing airborne intercepts, the copilot operated the radar in the rear cockpit. We performed the supersonic flight with full throttles and afterburner engaged from takeoff to thirty thousand feet and west of Tucson over the desert. With maximum power, it was essential that you kept the nose of the aircraft at a steep upward angle to avoid flying supersonic over Tucson. When you penetrated the sound barrier, the flight was so smooth that the only indication that you were flying at supersonic speed were the air speed indicator and the Mach indicator, which were superimposed on top of each other. After takeoff we would fly south close to the Mexican border and turn with a teardrop climb out back over Tucson. The old saying, if it can happen, it will happen was very true.

On a day off, I was in my quarters, and suddenly it sounded as if about three artillery shells had exploded in my apartment with dust flying all around me from the floor. This was a very good example of a crew that failed to stay zeroed on the air speed indicator when flying the supersonic mission. The crew had clearly broken the sound barrier and flew supersonic over the densely populated Tucson area. A big no-no due to the loud sonic booms that occur as you race over populated areas.

Later back at our home base in Holloman AFB, New Mexico, my counterparts were deploying to Vietnam. It was October 1965 when the 390th Squadron deployed to Da Nang. The 480th Squadron was deployed to Da Nang in December 1965. I was in Honolulu about five days on temporary duty to coordinate base functions as the 480th passed through.

Vietnam

The 391st Tactical Fighter Squadron deployed to Cam Ran Bay in late January 1966. This was the trip of a lifetime for me. My vice wing commander and I were tasked to be the control element for the fighter aircraft onboard the lead tanker with their tanker control element. We launched with ten tankers from March AFB in Riverside, California, and connected with our twenty fighters north of Los Angeles along the coast. The takeoff with a fully loaded tanker was a marvel at over three hundred thousand pounds gross weight, two hundred thousand pounds of fuel on board. The runway at March AFB Riverside, California, was about fourteen thousand feet long, and I could see the trees come into view before I observed the signal from the aircraft commander to his copilot to lift off. We made the first off-load north of Los Angeles and another couple of refueling hookups to get us to Honolulu. During the first off-load, I was with the boom operator in back and watched our aircraft as they moved into position to refuel. I waved pieces of fried chicken at them as they made their hookup. We had large containers of fried chicken onboard the tanker, and they were only permitted to carry a small box lunch onboard the fighter. I was sure they appreciated that gesture.

We were in Honolulu two days, and five more tankers were added to the ten we already had. The fifteen tankers carried enough fuel for the fighters to travel over six thousand miles nonstop on the next leg from Honolulu to Cam Ran Bay, Vietnam. We had only one tanker with an engine problem, and we directed the fighters to off-load all his fuel except enough for the tanker to land safely at Wake Island in the Pacific Ocean. We did not have any maintenance problems with any fighter aircraft on this trip.

It was a unique experience to look out of the tanker cockpit and see tankers and fighters line abreast right and left with each tanker with their assigned fighters about one mile apart almost as far as you could see. In 1966 this was just a routine operation compared to the initial efforts in the early 1950 period of midair refueling with the many heartbreaking growing pains. Can you imagine seeing a mass armada of thirty-four aircraft high over the Pacific Ocean, all fourteen tankers, and a total of twenty fighters line abreast with each tanker with their assigned fighters in loose formation meeting you in the air even if you are at a lower altitude, an awesome view that you will never forget during your lifetime. All aircraft flew off the very capable crew in the lead tanker. The fighters would takeoff directly after their assigned tanker. When the tankers performed the final refueling beyond the Philippine Islands, all fourteen returned to Guam. This final refueling gave the fighters enough fuel to reach their destination at Cam Ran Bay, Vietnam.

I deplaned from the tanker at Guam and rode on a transport to Clark AFB, Philippine Islands and from Clark to Cam Ran Bay by shuttle transport, and then to Phan Rang by boat. There were about seventy of us in an advanced party that lived in tents during the clearing of jungle foliage and construction of the air base. We made several trips to the air force headquarters at Ho Chi Minh City (Saigon) to obtain data and procedures for our headquarters and the 389th Fighter Squadron to begin operations as soon as they arrived on March 14, 1966. The bulldozers were working twenty-four hours each day with gunfire at them mostly at night, and they were very fortunate that no one was injured. We used sandbags stacked on top of one another adjacent to our tents for protection if we were under attack. The 101st Airborne Brigade was located next door to us. There were no attacks on the base until we were at Da Nang. On that attack my information was that none of the Vietnamese attackers survived, thanks to the fellows next door in the 101st Airborne Brigade.

The ramps and runways were constructed with aluminum sheets. Most of our missions here were close air support for ground units. This support included US Army, Marines, Korean Division, and Vietnamese troops. The Marine Division was located up near the South and North Vietnamese border, and they were the official greeters for the North Vietnam troops who illegally crossed the DMZ into South Vietnam.

The navy was experiencing heavy losses on their boat traffic up and down the rivers. The enemy would hide in the lush jungle tree growth and get the first shot and disable the potent gun on the boats. The organization conducting the defoliant spraying was named "Ranch Hand." At its peak in 1969 this organization had twenty-five spray aircraft. The UC-123 tactical transport known as "Patches" got its name the hard way. The aircraft was held together nose to tail with repairs to the battle damage inflicted by almost six hundred hits from enemy ground gunners in Vietnam. The total Ranch Hand force was 1269 pilots, navigators, flight mechanics, and ground personnel. During the tree-top-level spraying, the Ranch Hand air crews suffered a loss of twenty-seven people killed in action. The decision was made to spray the trees with the toxic herbicide, dioxin, also known as Agent Orange, that causes the leaves from the trees to fall to the ground in three days. The original delivery was at the very risky treetop level, but during my tour the level of spraying was at four thousand feet with two F-4C aircraft escorting at one mile behind and one mile to either side of the spraying aircraft.

The operation was so successful that it was used in most wooded areas all over the country.

At the time of the war, there was no information available on the horrific effects that this chemical has on humans. Fast-forward to 1991. Our government agreed to compensate those military personnel who had been exposed to the poisonous dioxin while serving in Vietnam. Much later, according to the Department of Veterans Affairs, the government acknowledged that many diseases were linked to dioxin exposure, including the following:

AL amyloidosis, chronic B-cell leukemias, chloracne, diabetes mellitus Type II, Hodgkins lymphoma, Ischemic heart disease, multiple myelomo, non-Hodgkins lymphoma, Parkinsons disease, peripheral neuropathy, porphyria cutanea tarda, prostate cancer, respiratory cancers, and soft tissue sarcomas. (These were listed in the January 2015 issue of the *Air Force Magazine*.)

In 2013, I read an article by a former army chaplain and his wife in the *Washington Post* magazine. In the article, the chaplain describes a vacation trip they made from Hanoi to Ho Chi Minh City in the south and a stopover at the old Da Nang air base. The chaplain stated that a recent test of the air surrounding the Da Nang air base indicated there were still very high levels of the dioxin present. They visited a nursery that was located near Da Nang with a large number of what are called Box Babies. The mothers and fathers of these children were both exposed to Agent Orange, and the children were born with no developed spinal cord. They would not ever be able to walk or use their arms. They were transported from one location to another in boxes. They indicated that some of our doctors were volunteering to travel over there and assist in the care of these very unfortunate children. This story is a tragic reminder of the lingering effects of the war.

Vietnam Afterthoughts

Back to wartime in Vietnam, I flew a number of missions with two F-4C aircraft as we escorted the C-123 aircraft while he was spraying the dioxin at four thousand feet. We flew about one mile behind and one mile to the left and right of the spaying aircraft. The UC-123 aircraft designation was for two jet engines added for heavy lift takeoff to the two-propeller engines.

One of the missions I was involved in was support for a company of marines, approximately two hundred personnel. They were surrounded by North Vietnamese regular troops. Another company of marines were sent to help them break free, and they were pushed back. I was called in with three aircraft. I had four 250-pound bombs, the number two aircraft had twenty-four 2.75 inch rockets, and number three aircraft was loaded with four cans of napalm. Each can contained four hundred gallons of this horrible weapon.

As we arrived in the area, the clouds were broken at 2500 feet. We had to deliver using a modified pattern below the clouds, and at this low altitude, the enemy elevated their mortars upward, and they exploded all around our pattern. We were very fortunate that no one was hit. In my conversation with the forward air controller, we decided to send in the aircraft with napalm and drop one can on the fence row with trees and bushes to hide in. The delivery was made with a speed of 420 knots and 50 feet above the trees. I was happy that I was airborne and not able to hear the screams of the burning enemy troops as they made their hasty exit as the burning Napalm consumed them.

When the napalm tank struck the ground, it exploded and splashed forward about seven hundred feet, burning everything in its path. It was sticky like jelly and clung to the human body or any object it came in contact with. All the remaining enemy soldiers made a rapid exit from the fence row out into the open field. This became like a canned shoot. We expended all our remaining weapons, and the marines opened up with all their guns on the running soldiers in the open field and other enemy soldiers who were in the circle around the marine positions. I was not sure of the number that escaped. I suspected that not many of the enemy soldiers were able to return to their home base on that day. This mission was one of only three where I could see solders running on the ground

High Flight—Stories of an Air Force Fighter Pilot

while we picked them off at this very low altitude. We were given credit for thirty-five KIAs (killed in action). At this point the marines were free to maneuver.

Most of our supplies came into Vietnam at Ho Chi Minh City (Saigon) or Cam Ranh Bay. Supplies were transported from Ho Chi Minh City on a road that runs northeast. These supply runs were accomplished with a large number of vehicles in a trail with a number of machine guns to provide cover for the entire train. About eighty miles northeast of Ho Chi Minh City was a large, troublesome wooded area alongside the road. A number of ambush strikes by the enemy were recorded here.

The army decided to deploy an ambush there. This became a rather large engagement. I was on alert with two aircraft, we were scrambled to assist, and two F-100 aircraft were called from another base. There were three helicopters with additional troops orbiting to the east of my pattern. The firing was heavy along the road from the enemy in the wooded area. The forward air controller in a light aircraft gave us our run in headings. The very low altitude at which he traveled to mark the target for us made him fair game for every enemy gunner on the ground, and their losses with their slower speed were heavier than ours in the F-4C. The air force forward air controller in most cases resided with the army unit he supported. In his backseat, he usually would have an army officer from the unit he supported.

We made our runs from the southeast, heading northwest at a ninety-degree angle to the road. The two F-100 aircraft ran their pattern parallel to the road from the northeast to the southwest, and when they were clear of the target, the forward air controller would clear our two aircraft onto the target. On one of my passes, as I pulled the trigger for the Gatling gun with the airplane vibrating from the gunfire, I observed something coming into the left side of my gun sight circle, which was a five-inch circle with a dot in the center. I released the trigger and looked out and saw a Red Cross rescue helicopter with wounded flying along the road, northeast, right through my firing path. Most of the heavy firing from the weapons on the ground was alongside this road for a distance of one to two miles, and this was where both friendly and enemy soldiers were dying. This young helicopter pilot was mistakenly flying right over a heavy combat area. Just one stray bullet into one of the rotating blades of the copter may have brought him down. I observed him until he was safely out of the firing area. With all the gunfire on both sides of the road, I was amazed that he made it out safely. Air to ground combat became violent and chaotic quickly as weapons were fired from all directions. Fire and smoke with the clatter of guns and bombs exploding was a sad and very frightening experience, one I will never forget.

Another harrowing incident that I recall was when the US Army was attempting to destroy some enemy troops who hid in a wooded area by placing a blocking force in the open field. Another strong force of army troops was moving through the woods in a near straight line, and when they would stop, they fired smoke rockets up through the trees so those of us in the air could determine their location and not drop a bomb on our guys.

On one of my passes here, as the five-hundred-pound bomb exploded, the forward air controller shouted, "Hold everything!"

This was an urgent call a fighter pilot did not want to hear. After a short investigation on the ground, the message came back from the forward air controller that the troops on the ground admitted that they had moved forward *after* they had fired their smoke rockets and one soldier was knocked off his feet with minor injuries from the bomb concussion. We continued the operation, knowing that we survived a close, potentially fatal, friendly fire incident.

To this day, our military has focused a great deal of effort to reduce the incidents of friendly fire, but they continue to occur. Some assumed with high-level computers and sophisticated electronics that this problem would go away. But we saw a recent case in Afghanistan where a coordinate with one wrong digit was transmitted from the ground by one of our Special Forces personnel to a bomber aircraft navigator flying above at an altitude of twenty thousand feet. The bomb fell near the position of the soldier who transmitted the request and injured the future president of Afghanistan, Hamid Karzai, and some of his troops.

There were some missions in South Vietnam that were very dangerous. I was on a mission with three aircraft about six miles from the Cambodian border. A shell came by my cockpit from the rear, close enough that had I reached out, I could have probably touched it. The enemy counted the passes we made to finish our bomb drops, thinking that we did not have any more weapons. The Vietnamese then fired at me from behind so that I could not see the shell coming and maneuver to avoid it. It was about the size of a softball with a fiery trail behind it. The angle and speed of the aircraft was what saved me from a direct hit. The gun was located in Cambodia. We had just finished dropping our last bomb load, but the enemy did not know that we were also equipped with the Gatling gun with 1200 rounds of twenty-millimeter shells onboard each aircraft. We paid a visit to Cambodia and made matchsticks out of the jungle, but we did not see any explosions. We assumed the gun was on wheels and was able to move under the jungle foliage.

The Gatling gun was one of our best weapons in the Vietnam War, capable of firing at a rate of six thousand rounds per minute. We would not fire the entire load at one time; we would typically fire about four hundred rounds each pass. This prevented the overheating of the gun. After this diversion in Cambodia, we did not have enough fuel to get back to our home base, so we landed at the base near Ho Chi Minh City. One aircraft had experienced a hydraulic leak. We remained there until the next day. We were loaded with weapons, the aircraft with the hydraulic leak was repaired, and that aircraft went on to fly a mission with us, and then all three aircraft and crew recovered at our home base of Phan Rang.

During this period the North Vietnamese were constructing a surface-to-air missile site in the DMZ. The river that terminated into the Tonkin Gulf on the eastern coast to Laos on the west was the border of North and South Vietnam. By international agreement, the DMZ was not authorized to have any military units located in or transported through it. We observed the construction until the missiles were ready to be installed and deployed four flights of aircraft to destroy the site. My flight of three aircraft was the fourth flight on the target.

We launched from Phan Rang and climbed to an altitude of thirty thousand feet. We were in the clouds the entire trip of 175 miles, maneuvering between the most intense thunderhead areas shown on radar. My copilot and I were in constant conversation about what we were seeing on our radar scopes. We were able to make very small changes of direction to avoid the most violent thunderheads. If large thunderheads were in your path, radar was the answer for a safe flight. Our flight was very smooth, and the two aircraft with me were able to fly close formation with no difficulty. When we arrived at the site, there was nothing visible except the immense cloud of smoke and dust covering the target. We dropped our bombs into the middle of the dust. Later a reconnaissance flight showed total destruction. The North Vietnamese never tried to repeat this construction.

There were some living quarters, concrete runways, and administrative buildings in use as we departed for Da Nang in September 1966. I had finished my two-year tour in the headquarters, and I was assigned as flight commander of "A" Flight in the 389th Squadron. This move joined our 366 headquarters with three of our original squadrons at Da Nang. In the operation from Da Nang, our exposure was elevated. The Da Nang missions were all over North Vietnam, or if the target was weathered in, we would divert to targets on the Ho Chi Minh Trail in Laos. I flew on about six missions at night from Da Nang on road reconnaissance. After takeoff we traveled over the Gulf of Tonkin, past the DMZ, then inbound to the coastal road north and flew about one hundred miles north over the road at four thousand feet to the ferry across a large bay similar size to our Chesapeake Bay in Maryland.

We performed this mission with two aircraft; with more than two aircraft during a night missions, the maneuvers increased the possibility of collision. The second aircraft, four miles behind, would stay in touch with the lead aircraft by radar with our exterior lights off and with a briefed clock position and base altitude in relation to the target. The specific

High Flight—Stories of an Air Force Fighter Pilot

details of this information were different on each mission and clearly defined in our briefing prior to launch. This procedure prevented the enemy from accurate tracking as we executed our weapons delivery pattern and gave us some element of safety from potential collision with each other in the very dark night.

As we traveled the road, if I observed something that looked suspicious, I would deploy a flare. The altitude of four thousand feet placed us above small arms fire, and at this altitude the parachute attached to the flare gave us time to expend our ordinance before the flare touched the ground. The super bright flares would light up an area about three miles in diameter. Over the bay, if a weapon-loaded boat was crossing the bay as soon as a flare was deployed, all hell would break loose. Shells of a large caliber would come at us, and it looked like a Fourth of July fireworks display. If the heavily loaded weapons boat was not crossing the bay when a flare was deployed, they would conserve ammunition and not fire. These locations, both the north area where the boat loaded and the south end where the boat unloaded, were the most heavily defended area with guns only in the southern area of North Vietnam. We lost a number of our aircraft there.

My friend Al Lurie "vacationed" in the Hanoi Hilton when he was shot down there about the time I arrived In Vietnam. On one mission over the south end of the bay when the weapons-loaded boat was crossing, I was violently maneuvering the aircraft to avoid a hit, and I ripped about twelve feet of the right wing off by pulling excessive g-forces. The aircraft was manageable, and I made a safe landing. This was a power-on approach.

We were ordered to fly with power-on landing approach because the jet engine required a couple of seconds to spool up when moving the throttle out of the idle position before positive thrust was available. In World War II, flying propeller-equipped planes made a 360-degree descending turn back around to the runway. We were using this same pattern with jets in Alaska. Some touched down short, and I was one of them. We were later ordered to fly what some World War II fighter jocks called a bomber pattern. This new procedure solved the two-second lag in the jet problem.

I recall another scary night mission involving the ferryboat transporting war materials from the northern regions of North Vietnam. Under thick jungle foliage, the Vietnamese would load the boat for the four-mile trip by river to the north end of the bay. On this mission, because of not being able to see through the jungle foliage, I decided to punch off one five-hundred-pound bomb into the area where I thought the loading dock might be located. As soon as the bomb exploded, a massive number of guns on the ground fired at us. My copilot shouted that he could see an unguided rocket coming toward us from the rear. I violently maneuvered the aircraft, and for one brief moment, we were bottom side up in the dark. If I had turned off all my cockpit instrument lights, I would still have been able to read all my instruments from the light of the constant shell explosions directly behind us. We did not get a shell hit on either of our aircraft. I believe we came close to where the boat was anchored or where the material was stored until it was loaded onto the ferryboat.

In the Hanoi and Haiphong areas, the missiles overlapped in a seventy-mile radius in each of these locations. When these missile sites were being constructed, the F-105 aircraft was deployed, but our government would not let them destroy the sites while under construction for fear that the Russians were involved. There were about eight hundred F-105 aircraft in the inventory, and almost half of them were lost in Vietnam. They were the first deployed in 1965 and did a super performance until the F-4 arrived to assist them in late 1965. The F-105 was called "the Thud" by our pilots, and their pilots called the F-4 "the Lead Sled." Not destroying the missile sites during construction resulted in heavy losses of the F-105 and later the F-4. The enemy's SA-2 guideline thirty-five-foot-long "flying telephone pole" missiles had an effective range of about twenty-one miles, streaking toward a target at more than four times the speed of sound. It could fly up to an altitude of ninety thousand feet to deliver a 430-pound fragmentation warhead that could shred anything within its nearly three-hundred-yard maximum blast radius.

High Flight—Stories of an Air Force Fighter Pilot

In 1960, an SA-2 brought down Francis Gary Powers' U-2 reconnaissance aircraft over the Soviet Union. Seven years later in Vietnam, an SA-2 knocked off the right wing of John McCain's A-4 Skyhawk aircraft after he launched from a carrier in the Gulf, forcing him to eject into enemy territory, and he unfortunately spent an extended period of time in the prison camp. Missiles would launch, and if the target managed to escape, the engine would burn out, and the missile would automatically explode at fifty-two seconds after launch. Big guns and missiles were a severe threat in this area. It would be bad news for you if you were above the clouds and the missile popped up out of the clouds underneath your aircraft. If you could see the missile some distance away, you could maneuver violently to avoid it.

As I was finishing my tour, I flew one aircraft with a missile notification instrument installed on the lower left side of the instrument panel forward of my left knee. The instrument had a needle that pointed to the missile's direction from you, and a red light illuminated when the missile was locked on to my aircraft. You maneuvered your aircraft until the missile was arriving off the left or right wing of your aircraft and then dived or climbed. This maneuver avoided a hit. There were some heavy losses until this missile-detection equipment was installed. The two MIG bases located in Vietnam were at the northern city limits of Hanoi and about forty-five miles southwest. It was a guessing game if and when they were to launch or not. I did not see one MIG in the air on my tour, but I could see them on the ramps of the air bases. We were not permitted to attack unless they were airborne and approaching us in a hostile manner.

Another mission was with two F-4C aircraft providing protection and escort of the RB-66. The RB-66 had about fourteen technicians onboard to operate the radar-jamming equipment that targeted the enemy radar as the strike force passed underneath our pattern. The RB-66 pattern was beyond the reach of the missiles. We could see them exploding a very short distance to the east of our location. Our patterns were a racetrack with one RB-66 with two F-4C aircraft at the Chinese border and the other RB-66 with escorts 150 miles south. When we headed south from the Chinese border, we would meet the other RB traveling north about six miles off our left as the strike force passed underneath.

One incident occurred when a pilot friend was at the Chinese border. As they flew their pattern two miles on either side of the RB-66, and one mile behind, he looked to his left and a MIG-21 was closing fast on the RB-66. My friend rolled to his left and behind the MIG, shot him down just before the MIG was in firing position on the RB-66. Then the two other MIGs above their altitude came down and entered the fight. My friend maneuvered behind one MIG, and the MIG pilot decided it might be safer to motor home at a very high rate of speed. Our aircraft chased after the MIG about eighty miles into China. As the MIG slowed down to land at his home base, our aircraft closed in on the MIG and shot him down. He came back into Vietnam without any competition. He was given credit only for the MIG he shot down in Vietnam, not for the one that he chased into China. At this time, the political direction was for us not to engage any fighters in China or fly over the border into Cambodia. There were exceptions for hot pursuit.

There were Russian and Chinese forces at the two bases, and some were flying in the MIG aircraft. I flew a few night missions in Laos on the Ho Chi Minh Trail. One of the most memorable was with my two aircraft, fully loaded with ordinance, flying at four thousand feet in an orbit around the C-130 gunship as it blasted trucks on the road below. They had equipment to see the trucks at night, and we could see the blast upon impact. The C-130 operated with about sixteen personnel manning the one large gun and a number of mini Gatling guns and with all guns firing at once, eighteen thousand rounds per minute. The C-130 was a very potent weapon system with excellent firepower. Our mission was to assist the rescue crews in the event the C-130 was shot down.

A Fateful Day

December 2, 1966, is a day etched firmly in my memory. Our strike mission was on the oil and fuel tanks adjacent to Phuc Yen Airfield on the northern city limits of Hanoi. This was the first time we were ordered to strike near this airfield with a major direction center located on the base. The mission was briefed with all aircrews for both the strike and MIG cap going into Hanoi. I was the spare for the flight that fellow pilots and friends, Don Burns and Bruce Ducat, were number three in a flight of four aircraft. All flights into the area of potential MIG activity had four aircraft in each flight. If we encountered MIGS, we would fight in flights of two aircraft, a leader and wingman. We taxied five aircraft to the arming pad at the end of the runway. Had anyone aborted for any malfunction, I was the spare for this fateful flight.

On takeoff, we flew west for about one hour to northeastern Thailand, joined a tanker to top off our fuel tanks. We then headed north to about seventy miles northwest of Hanoi, turned to 120 degrees toward Hanoi, and descend to twelve thousand feet flying above what became known as "Thud Ridge," located along the Red River. Sadly it was called "Thud Ridge" because of the high volume of F-105 aircraft that were shot down and crashed there. When the target passed under the nose of the aircraft, you rolled the aircraft bottom side up and pulled the aircraft nose down until you observed the target in line with the nose of your aircraft. This was a very accurate forty-five-degree dive angle. Next you rolled upright and dived to 7,500 feet at 420 knots, tracking the target with your gun sight. At 7,500 feet, you released the bombs and performed a four "G" pull, and the aircraft would level at about four thousand feet. Four thousand feet was our magic number to avoid the small arms fire from the ground.

During the Vietnamese war, we had to visually see the target; a few years later, there were vast improvements in electronics and delivery procedures, but more on this later. We established spacing during the bomb delivery of about one-quarter mile between aircraft. After delivery, we used near full throttle, maintaining the spacing by "jinking" the aircraft, which was moderate right and left turns, until we were out of the high-threat area.

During this mission our flight of four aircraft was the only flight to strike the target; the rest of the force aborted because of poor weather. After delivery of the weapons, our flight was in trail and near the max range of the missile threat when the aircraft commander in aircraft number four saw two missiles pass over his aircraft, and one smashed into the tailpipe of Don Burns' aircraft, severing the tail. These two missiles engines had already burned out, which indicated that in just a few seconds later, the missiles would have exploded at a safe distance. Burns was picked up in a rice paddy by several Vietnamese women armed with pitchforks and was later stripped and abused for several hours and then was driven to the camp in Hanoi where he remained captive for about seven years. Our squadron received notification that Burns was a prisoner six months after the shoot down, but we never received any status on Bruce Ducat until the prisoners were released seven years later. Bruce Ducat was apparently shot and killed during the pickup in the wooded area, and when the prisoners were released, his body was returned in a metal box. I met with Burns years later, and his experience in the prison camp was very difficult.

On these missions up north, we knew by ten o'clock the night before where our targets were the next day. This gave us plenty of time to think about it as we were awake and in the restroom at 3:00 a.m. the next morning shaving among vomit on the floor. Some pilots got sick just thinking about the unknown factors in their upcoming missions. We finished our briefings and were in the cockpit at 6:00 a.m. At the moment the canopy closed, the adrenaline started pumping, and you knew there was no turning back and that tactics you had been trained to execute must come forth. My final mission was in the early-morning hours of December 20, 1966. I was relieved to be going home to my family but overwhelmed with sadness that we had lost so many of my colleagues and that we had to leave behind many in horrible conditions at the North Vietnamese prisons.

In my twenty-seven years in the air force, I met and served with some of the most competent and loyal men who I have ever known. I have sympathy for the families of those we lost. And I can't describe the feeling I have for the crew members who were in the prison camp five to seven years with abuse and torture almost every day. Our Senator John

High Flight—Stories of an Air Force Fighter Pilot

McCain can give anyone an extensive briefing on this horrible treatment. According to Senator McCain, very often he was tortured by captors who handcuffed his arms behind his back and then rotated his arms up and hung the handcuffs on a meat hook on the wall so that his feet did not touch the floor for hours. This maneuver will dislocate your shoulder joints and with no medical treatment provided.

Heavy enemy fire could be catastrophic on an aircraft. A direct hit on an aircraft by a very large shell would incinerate both crew members and aircraft into very small, unidentifiable pieces. I recall that, at a later date, an acquaintance of mine had a brother who was the pilot who was most likely shot down with a very large shell in the same area where I ripped the twelve feet of my aircraft wing off from very violent maneuvering. This was the same location where the radar signature of their aircraft was last observed. About three searches were made between 1970 and 1990 in this area, and nothing identifiable was found.

Our armed forces search and recovery crews were the best ever. Some were in helicopters, some were in navy submarines or destroyers along the North Vietnam coast, some were in tanker aircraft and one of our own F-4C pilots ordered his wingman to lower his tail hook, and he connected his forward wind screen with the tail hook of his wingman and pushed him about eighty miles to a safe location where both crews were able to eject. The wingman's aircraft was full of holes, and all of his fuel leaked out. The flight leader did not have enough fuel after pushing a very heavy aircraft for that distance and had no tanker or air base within range for fuel, and he ejected.

On another distress call, a tanker crew heard a call of another pilot with many holes in his aircraft, and the tanker crew, with total disregard for their own safety, rushed into hostile territory and provided him with the fuel to reach a safe area. These are true stories of real, live heroes and those who died during rescue attempts who probably never received honors or credit for their valor.

Another instance of bravery I recall is when several young men died as two helicopters were shot down in the process of rescuing an F-105 pilot after his aircraft was shot down near the DMZ. They apparently were in the middle of an ambush. This recovery was turned over to two civilians, an American and a Vietnamese. This was a very high-risk operation as they were dressed as Vietnamese fishermen with the large hats that covered their faces. They entered the river that formed the border for North and South Vietnam from the Gulf of Tonkin at night. As they traveled west on the river, they were challenged by illegal North Vietnamese outposts in the zone, and each time only the Vietnamese would respond that they were fishermen going out to harvest fish from their lines. No one from any of the outposts came out to investigate. They were permitted to continue.

The F-105 pilot they were attempting to rescue was an avid golfer, and he had been briefed on his emergency radio in golf terminology that would place him on the edge of the river. When the rescue crew arrived at this point, they made a brief radio transmission, and the pilot ran out of the dark and jumped into their boat. They placed him flat on the bottom of the boat and covered him with a blanket and brought him all the way back to the Tonkin Gulf to safety. These two men placed themselves in a position where they were in grave danger of losing their own lives to rescue the F-105 pilot. I have read some articles written by this F-105 pilot about how grateful he was to these two very brave men for what they did for him. Had they not recovered him, he would have been in a North Vietnamese prison or dead.

Another dramatic nighttime rescue occurred when one of our aircraft was hit over the southern part of the bay ferry and it was engulfed in flames. The copilot was close to the fire in the rear cockpit and was telling the aircraft commander that it was getting hot in the backseat. In the darkness with little visibility, the aircraft commander was trying to get past the shore line and over the water. His copilot suddenly ejected, and the aircraft commander, thinking the aircraft was falling apart, rapidly pulled the ejection device between his knees while leaning forward and severely damaged three of his vertebrae. The recommended procedure was to sit straight upright and reach up above your head with both hands and pull the two circular medal rings forward and down over your face.

This activated the ejection sequence. The rocket attached to the back side of the pilot seat provided the upward power for the seat and pilot to clear a damaged aircraft by a safe distance. This very powerful rocket seat could damage your back unless you were in the upright position as indicated above. These two pilots were fortunate as they were picked up by the navy ships offshore. Some of the offshore pickups became a gun duel with shore batteries firing until the navy ship fired a few big gun shots, and then silence. The actions of some of the crews during rescue efforts were far beyond the call of duty. It was a good feeling to know that these young men were on alert and ready to launch when the large shells and missiles were passing close by.

Lessons Learned

During this war, our Army, Navy, Marines, Coast Guard, National Guard, and the Air Force, along with their civilian counterparts, were, and still are without a doubt, the most capable fighting team ever assembled in our history. We may throw darts at one another during peacetime, but the color of the uniform is of no consequence when you are under attack. As a team we move forward in lockstep.

Since the Vietnam War, our American armed forces have been pulled into many other conflicts around the world. We have seen a quantum leap forward in the technology and accuracy of our weapons and aircraft since the 1960s. These advances have made a huge difference in the injuries and deaths of our troops in combat. Today we can aim a smart bomb or missile into the window or chimney of a building with startling accuracy. And thanks to satellites and drones, we can now see the enemy from the safety of thousands of miles away. In stark contrast, during World War II, historians estimate that about 25 percent of all bombs released hit the intended target. Today, estimates are that over 90 percent of missiles and smart bombs strike the intended target.

I learned a lot of valuable lessons from the school of hard knocks in Vietnam. As a fighter pilot, one of the most important ones was to never press beyond the design g-force limits of aircraft, except of course in combat. Also keep in mind, practice makes perfect! One of the reasons our American air force was superior was the amount of repetitious training our pilots received. It was important to respect the environment you flew in, the aircraft, and your own capability. Pride and arrogance had no place in a cockpit.

The high standards for all fighter pilots were established in World War II by the British during the air battle that prompted Hitler not to invade England and by American fighter pilot victories like Major Bong's forty air force victories in a P-38 aircraft.

One RAF fighter pilot who stood alone above many others was Douglas Bader. About 1935 he was injured in an accident and lost his foot and leg just below the knee. He was fitted with a prosthetic leg and foot. At this time the RAF elected to retire him. As the war was coming close to British soil, they made a decision to allow Douglas back into active service. Soon after he was back as a fighter pilot, he experienced another accident with an injury that caused him to lose the other leg and foot. Now he had two prosthetic legs below the knees. He had very unique talents as a fighter pilot and was permitted to remain on duty and became a squadron commander during the very successful air battle that caused Hitler to cancel his invasion plans against England and redirect his armies east to invade Russia. Two pilots who were in his squadron were Robert Tuck and Jeffrey Paige. When the Germans almost had the French on the ropes, Churchill requested that Robert Tuck fly him over to France after dark in an attempt to strengthen the French will to fight, and return to London before daylight the next morning. This effort failed, and the French threw in the towel, and within about one week they surrendered.

Shortly after the surrender, Germany had heavy antiaircraft guns along the coastline of France. Douglas Bader was on a fighter mission along the coast of France and was shot down. He was able to separate from the aircraft, and when he landed on his prosthetic legs, they were destroyed. He became a German prisoner of war. The Germans were so thrilled with his guts and determination to perform his part on behalf of his country that they sent the British a wire message that they would assure safety for an aircraft on a specific day and at a specific time and place to transport and drop a set of new prosthetic legs. The British complied, and Douglas survived the prison experience and returned home.

Forty-five years later, in Washington, DC, his daughter Virginia Bader was selling World War II paintings of American aircraft severely damaged and returning from battle. To help her draw a large number of potential buyers, she invited Robert Tuck and Jeffrey Paige to join her. I attended this sale and was able to talk at great length with both of these heroic fighter pilots. Robert Tuck gave us a very good description of how he squeezed Prime Minister Churchill into the very small storage space behind the pilot position on his fighter aircraft. I decline to get into the details, but I am still laughing at his description of the account! On another occasion the prime minister stated that the fighter pilot's mission was hours and hours of boredom punctuated by moments of "stark terror." I agreed this was a pretty accurate description of a fighter pilot's life.

Jeffrey Paige was from the Handley Paige Aircraft manufacturing family. He became a fighter pilot and was assigned to Douglas Bader's squadron. In the propeller-equipped aircraft, the engine was forward of the pilot. In a jet fighter, the engines were all behind us. Jeffrey was on a mission along the French coast and was hit with gunfire in the engine area. The Germans at this time had control of one half of the English Channel. Jeffrey was determined not to bail out over the German side of the channel, and his burns from the forward engine fire and the wind stream directing the flames right into his cockpit were heavy. He made the distance to the English-controlled area and climbed out of the heavily damaged aircraft and was rescued by friendly British sailors. He had severe burns all over his body, and when I spoke with him, he stated that he had experienced forty surgeries to get rid of keloids from his injuries. The surgeries promoted mobility in his fingers and other body joints by grafting healthy skin from other parts of his body to the affected areas. To me, it was a great thrill to meet and talk to these British fighter pilots who paved the way for later fighter pilots like me. It was an honor to hear their harrowing combat accounts firsthand.

After the Vietnamese war, the US Air Force established a simulated combat training area over the desert north of Las Vegas, Nevada, known as "Red Flag." All segments of this activity were heavily computerized. The war games were conducted up to three times each year, using a small contingent of ground troops and each type of aircraft used in potential future conflicts from each of our military services. On some occasions, we also had representatives from NATO, Japan, and Australia join in our training operations.

With all elements of the training activity heavily computerized, supervisors on the air base could monitor screens of aircraft and other training assets as they performed air-to-air and air-to-ground maneuvers, and when they returned, the supervisors could show them on the screen their incorrect maneuvers and the mistakes that they needed to correct. There were many simulated radar missile firing locations several miles apart in the desert that could fire a simulated missile at a low-flying aircraft and record a direct hit or a near miss measured in feet.

I was on a visit to one of these simulated missile firing sites, and I was amazed at the advanced training capability this exercise provides. It had been estimated that in past conflicts the first ten missions were where we experienced the largest air losses. If the pilot survived the first ten missions, then he would probably survive the entire conflict. The Red Flag was the air force's means to provide those critical first ten missions in a controlled, peacetime environment. According the air force, the approximately $35 million allocated each year on this training was well spent. There was also a Red Flag training capability in Alaska to train in cold weather operations. These computerized training tools, the latest engine technology, and advanced aerodynamics is why I believe the US Air Force is second to none.

The Pentagon Years

After completing my final combat mission in the early-morning hours, I departed Vietnam late afternoon on December 20, 1966, with an assignment to air force headquarters located at the Pentagon. I served as a computer analyst for two years, and then I was promoted to chief of the Operation Data Branch. I was promoted to lieutenant colonel in 1967 and into a position to manage twenty-five airmen and four officers in a twenty-four-hour operation. We received and updated all combat reports, including the status of conventional and nuclear forces. All of these reports were updated into our state-of-the-art IBM computers. We distributed the reports the next morning to units throughout the Pentagon and to those in the field.

I was promoted to full colonel in 1971 and departed the Pentagon for an assignment to Tactical Air Command located at Hampton, Virginia. When I arrived at TAC, the automation activity consisted of three separate systems—operations, intelligence, and comptroller. My job was chief of the Operation Branch. I had eighty computer programmers and analysts reporting to me. At this time there was a massive expansion of computers into all areas of the air force, including aircraft. Interoperability and consolidation was a must for all systems to be capable of passing data to other services and the Joint Chiefs of Staff. This was required because most of our actions in our worldwide commitments were with elements of all US services and in some cases service members of other nations. We gave the commander of Tactical Air Command a briefing that recommended that all computer activity at the headquarters be consolidated under a single manager. The general approved.

We organized the three activities under the Chief Office of Data Automation. We organized four subordinate units: Plans Division, Intelligence Division, Tactical Division, and Comptroller Division. This action consolidated five hundred programmers and analysts into one unit. From 1972 to 1975, I was chief of the Tactical Division. From 1975 to 1977, I was promoted to chief, Office of Data Automation. I supervised one thousand personnel, five hundred at TAC Headquarters and another five hundred at eighteen bases in the United States and Panama. We provided computer support to eighty thousand personnel in the command.

In January 1977 I received a telephone call from personnel, inquiring if I would accept an assignment to NATO Headquarters located in Brussels, Belgium. I declined for family reasons.

I retired on June 30, 1977, with twenty-seven years of service, one combat tour with 150 combat missions. Decorations and medals include the Legion of Merit for Administrative Supervision at Tactical Air Command Headquarters, the Distinguished Flying Cross for a mission in Vietnam, Meritorious Service Medal for Administrative Supervision of Personnel in the Pentagon, and seven Air Medals for the 150 combat missions.

My retirement was a bittersweet time for me and my family. While I felt it was the right time to step away from public service, I also knew I would miss all the amazing men and women I served proudly with all those years. And all the high flying adventures up in the clouds. Those same clouds that I would gaze at from the safety of our simple cotton farm in Alabama. Where my story truly began…

Humble Beginning

I was born May 10, 1928, on a farm two miles northeast of Rogersville, Alabama. At that time, Rogersville was a small town with a population of approximately four hundred people. I attended elementary school from 1934 to 1940. I attended Lauderdale County High School and graduated in 1947. My parents, James Donie and Katie Bedingfield Romine purchased our sixty-acre farm in 1926. A generous neighbor named Peter Cox held the farm mortgage. In 1929, when the financial system collapsed, Mr. Cox assured my dad that he would not foreclose if we were unable to pay either the interest or principle on the loan. A shining example of how the kindness and generosity of our neighbors made a tremendous impact on our family's life. We survived the tough times, but many families did not. My maternal grandmother, Frances Bedingfield, passed away in 1935, and my mother's share of her estate was a forty-acre plot. Proceeds from the sale of this land were used to reduce the mortgage.

High Flight—Stories of an Air Force Fighter Pilot

My mother, Katie, gave birth to ten children; only seven males grew up as adults. Two little girls, one about four and the other at one year old passed away in the early 1920s. Their deaths were caused by an unknown disease and lack of modern medication. The third was a little boy stillborn in 1935.

My oldest brother, Henry, started his career as an educator, and then in the 1940s, he served in the Alabama State Legislature for four years. It is interesting that, during his time in the legislature, the local road was paved and electricity became available in our house. The two brothers next in line were James and Stanley, who both worked with the Tennessee Valley Authority. Stanley also became a pipe fitter, and on one of his assignments he was located at Oak Ridge, Tennessee. He stated that they were placing interior nickel-coated pipes into the buildings. We did not know for what purpose this facility was developed, but later data was released that Oak Ridge was one of three large facilities that contributed to the development of the atom bomb.

Years later while stationed at Holloman Air Force Base near Alamogordo, New Mexico, in 1963, two of my friends and I were coyote hunting about forty-five miles north of Alamogordo, New Mexico, and we walked through the area where the first atom bomb test was exploded in 1945. We picked up melted sand that became glass particles. Recently the location was declared a tourist site with fences and roads into the area for visitors.

The four younger brothers were James Donie also known as J. D. Jr., Douglas, me, and the youngest brother, Bobby. J. D. graduated from pilot and single-engine fighter training in March 1945; he was then assigned for two years of occupation duty in the Philippine Islands. He was released from the air force in 1947, and then he earned a degree in aeronautical engineering at Auburn University. He worked on the B-36 Bomber design in Fort Worth, Texas, for about three years and then transferred to the Lockheed Transport Division in Marietta, GA. At this location he worked on the design for the C-5, C-141, C-140, and the C-130 for approximately thirty-five years until his retirement. Douglas was in the navy during World

War II in New York City. He contacted spinal meningitis with severe aftereffects. In those days most with this disease never survived. I was next in age and then my younger brother, Bobby, who served in the US Navy for twenty years. At this writing, just my older brother J. D. and I are the remaining living brothers.

My mother's maiden name was Bedingfield. When she was a teenager in 1900, her father and twenty-one-year-old brother were shot on the same day while they were hauling logs to the saw mill on separate wagons. Both died a few days apart from this escalating feud. The killer escaped to Arkansas and was bragging about killing two people in Alabama. He was arrested and returned to Alabama for trial and was convicted. He was on a road gang, as it was common for prisoners to work, clean up, and repair roads in those days. It appeared that he had assistance to escape by his guards. He vanished, never to be heard from again. This was a heartache for my mother for the rest of her days.

Living on a farm during the Depression was not easy; however my parents instilled in us good work habits and independence. We had our own blacksmith shop where we could sharpen or repair tools, implements, and harnesses. Some kids had a store-bought little red wagon, but my dad built a wagon made of wood that had wheels and a tongue to steer that we could ride on. We had plenty to eat, since we grew and canned vegetables from our very large garden, and we also canned meat from the farm.

In the early years on the farm, we did not have electricity or central heat. On cold nights, we used heavy quilts that the neighborhood women had sewn by hand during their many quilting parties. I remember getting off the school bus, and they were in our house sewing, talking and having a great time.

Alabama summers were very hot and humid, and our farmhouse did not have central air conditioning. We used open windows and fans to cool things off.

During the spring, usually in April, tornadoes were very common. In 1936, a tornado blew away Tupelo, Mississippi, located about sixty miles southwest of Rogersville. I was eight years old at that time. We were awakened at 1:00 a.m. that morning with very strong winds and constant bright flashes of lightning. Our home was rocking and rolling from the strong winds. I recall my mother telling us to put all our clothes on so "that we would not go into the hereafter undressed." An interesting sidebar to this recollection is that Elvis Presley and his family survived the destruction at Tupelo.

Our original house, probably built in the 1920s, was a two-level structure. The interior of the house was divided into eight spacious rooms, with a hall for the stairs to the second floor. Each room, including the hallway and pantry adjoining the kitchen, were all finished, wall and ceiling with tongue and groove pine. The pine was its beautiful natural color. We had four bedrooms for six people at the time; my three older brothers were grown and on their own. The house was orientated east and west with a fireplace and brick chimney at each end. The dining room and kitchen were connected to the living room on the east end of the house. This was an L-shaped house. There were wraparound porches on each side of the house, and the ceilings of the porches were of the same pine that was in the interior of the house. This very roomy house burned to the ground in 1940. The pine burns rapidly, as it would have if soaked with gasoline. We were able to get one bed out. No one was injured, but our dog lost his hair and suffered a few wounds, but he survived. We think the fire was started from a bird nest located too near the kitchen stove funnel at the exit of the funnel to the roof from the second floor.

We lost everything in the house fire, but what happened there after is worthy of recording. The neighbors throughout the countryside pitched in and collected more canned food and other items than we had before. One of my classmates had a little wagon and a pony for transportation, and he contributed to the effort. But to top everything that had already been contributed, my mother's first cousin had recently purchased everything needed to construct a house for his son. He gave my family all the material to construct a new three-bedroom house. In the building process, most of the labor was volunteer. Labor was cheap, fifty cents per day, or room and board for one person was fifteen dollars per month. Our new home was built in 1940 on the same spot where the original farmhouse was located. Electricity and indoor plumbing came soon after to our home.

Work in the fields was with mule or horsepower to pull the many implements. Our cash crop was cotton, only five cents per pound during the Depression; however in late 1930 when the war in Europe increased the demand for cotton products, the price increased to forty or fifty cents per pound. The farm mortgage was paid in full at this time. During my time, cotton was picked manually, a very labor-intensive and exhausting job. I recall how the cotton boll, when fully open, would cut my fingers as I reached in to pull out the cotton. The maximum amount picked manually by one person was about three hundred pounds per day. Today large machines pick the cotton. Our farm was sold to another family in the 1970s and is now part of a large beef cattle farm. Cotton is still farmed in Rogersville at other farms.

In addition to cotton, we grew our own vegetables and fruit, which we canned with the steam pressure cooker. We had plenty of fish to eat, since we were about one mile from a spring-fed branch, and it emptied into Anderson Creek about two miles from our location. Anderson Creek connected into the Elk River about three miles downstream, and the Elk River terminated into the mighty Tennessee River about four miles from our location. My dad constructed a canoe with wood to be used for fishing and filled the potential leaks with cotton and heated tar. When the heated tar cooled and hardened, it sealed all the water leaks.

The Tennessee River was an important part of the economy and life in this area of Alabama. The Tennessee Valley Authority was established in the early 1930s at the direction of President Roosevelt. This organization is responsible for construction and maintenance of the dams and the locks for cargo and recreational boat traffic to navigate up and down the river. There is one exception, and that is Wilson Dam. The construction of Wilson Dam by the Army Corps of Engineers was begun in 1918 to generate electrical power for a nitrate plant to be used in explosives during

World War I. The dam was completed in 1924, and the army engineers who constructed the dam continue to be responsible for maintenance and operation of the dam and lock used for boat traffic. The proposal to make navigation on the Tennessee River practical ensues from the fact that this district is rich in natural resources, mineral, timber, and agricultural.

Also, it had long been realized that the 140-foot drop in the short stretch from Decatur, Alabama, to Florence, Alabama, in the river was capable of producing abundant and cheap power. The Wilson Dam was 137 feet high and contained thirty-six million cubic feet of masonry. The local newspaper also stated that this amount of masonry was sufficient to construct a concrete boulevard sixty-four feet wide and six inches thick from New York City to Washington, DC. This was one of four of the largest dams located on the river. Several smaller dams were in the Knoxville area. The first large dam was located at Guntersville, Alabama. Pickwick Landing Dam was the fourth of the large dams, and it was located just to the north of the Tennessee state line, in the vicinity of where a very large Civil War battle occurred.

The two big dams near Rogersville were Wheeler, about four miles west of my home, and about fifteen miles farther west was the Wilson Dam near Florence, Alabama. Each of these dams measures approximately one mile long from bank to bank. The space between the Wheeler and Wilson Dams during the time when the American Indians were living in the area was named Muscle Shoals because of the giant boulders in the water and lots of muscle power required to maneuver canoes through the swift water.

The dams were a very important part of our lives in Rogersville during that time. When I was a thirteen-year-old boy in 1941, our government was walking a tightrope to avoid the war in Europe that started in the late 1930s. I have a vivid recollection of Sunday, December 7, 1941, at 1:00 p.m. when a friend drove into our driveway and shouted that the Japanese had bombed Pearl Harbor. The following day, all of us high school students gathered in the auditorium to listen by radio to President Roosevelt's declaration of war, his famous "a day that will live in infamy" speech. It was evident from documents later available that Germany and Japan were planning to conquer the world and divide it into two large empires. For a teenager, it was frightening to hear of this war, even though it was thousands of miles away.

About two or three days after Pearl Harbor, Germany declared war on the United States. Our government was reading the messages of Japan before the attack, but it required about three days for our experts to fully understand and translate the content. This process after Pearl Harbor was reduced to a matter of hours. The British had access to one of the German code machines from a German aircraft crash in Yugoslavia. A unit loyal to the British picked up the burned pieces of the code machine and passed it over to the British, at the same time placing burned and twisted pieces of metal in the wreckage to convince the Germans that their machine was completely destroyed. The British were able to reconstruct the machine. This capability was shared with our government, and our military had access to the German messages during the war.

I was fascinated by the war events as a teenager and began reading newspapers and books about Pearl Harbor after the attack and learned that the Japanese navy admiral, Isoroku Yamamoto, who led the attack on Pearl Harbor, had spent a great deal of time in the United States as a young military officer in the Diplomatic Corp. After the attack he stated that he feared that the Japanese had just "awakened a sleeping giant." It appeared that he was not in total agreement with his political leaders.

In April 1943 as we read the Japanese messages, we became aware of the itinerary of Admiral Yamamoto visit to their conquered Pacific islands. At this time the admiral was chief of the Japanese Combined Fleet. American P-38 fighter aircraft did not normally have the range to get to any one of the islands on his visit. The maintenance personnel installed drop fuel tanks and attached them to the wings. The fuel in these tanks was used immediately after takeoff, and then the tanks were jettisoned into the sea to reduce drag on the aircraft. This mission was indicated as a million to one chance of success. They launched about fifteen P-38 fighters from Guadalcanal to intercept the admiral and his deputy before they landed at the Bougainville Island base in two separate aircraft. This flight was successful; they used expert navigation and arrived at the same time as the admiral and his deputy were entering the traffic pattern for landing and shot down both of their aircraft with one P-38 loss. This was the longest successful intercept recorded during the war. This mission was approved by the president of the United States, and he wired his congratulations to the fighter pilots after the mission. The P-38J was the aircraft model flown by Major Richard Bong, America's highest-scoring ace of all time with forty victories during World War II.

Before we entered the war, President Roosevelt bypassed the neutral Congress, giving the British war material and ships by labeling the transaction as Lend-Lease. The president also performed a number of actions that made the country better equipped in case war came to pass. He gave grants to colleges all over the country to establish aviation courses with light aircraft available for flight instructions at the colleges. The president also directed our industries to increase the total number of bombers and fighters produced each year and increased the number of barracks and other facilities to train large numbers of soldiers. All these facilities experienced major expansions after our country entered the war, and the plants manufacturing war weapons and material went on a twenty-four-hour, around-the-clock operation. The plants near my home produced sheets of aluminum by the Reynolds Aluminum Company, and these sheets were used as skin on aircraft, and the fertilizer normally manufactured by another company produced nitrate that was used in bombs and shells. Gasoline was rationed, a specific amount to each family. Buses picked up the workers from all over the countryside and transported them to the plants for the three eight-hour shifts.

For the first time in our history, women were a very important element of the work force in aircraft production and almost all other plants manufacturing war material. This was the time of Rosie the Riveter. Our nation surprised the world with the staggering amount of war material and weapons we shipped to England and Russia while still having enough for our own military. The draft system used to fill the ranks of the military was terminated in March 1945. Two months later I was eighteen years old, and I did not serve in World War II.

After the war ended, I enrolled in Florence State Teachers College in 1947 through 1949. It later became the North Alabama University at Florence. I became friends with several of the students who were in the Merchant Marines during World War II. They were members of a naval reserve unit located on the Tennessee River. I joined the unit to hear of their war experiences. They were members on ship convoys of twenty or more ships moving war material across the North Atlantic to England and Russia. On some trips up to half of the ships were sunk. If your ship was sunk there was no searching for survivors for fear of losing another ship to German submarines surrounding the convoy. The convoy just moved ahead with full throttles; they suffered some of the heaviest losses during the early part of the war.

In 1949 I transferred to Auburn University to pursue a bachelor's degree. The Korean War began in 1950, and the naval reserve unit I was assigned to was in the process of being called to active duty. I was in contact with the air force recruiters for pilot training in the air force. I passed the written and later the physical exam. I chose the air force over the navy because I loved airplanes and I wanted to fly. I had flown a number of flights with a high school classmate, Norman Cosby, in his all-metal Luscombe two-seat aircraft, performing spins, rolls, and loops. We did not use parachutes in those days; we were convinced that nothing tragic could happen to us. Favor was on my side.

I was pilot in the following aircraft:

For pilot training: T-6, T-28, B-25 propeller equipped.

For the jets: T-33, F-80, F-94B, F-94C, TF-102, F-102, F-84F, F-4C Phantom II (150 combat missions in Vietnam), and the T-39 at Langley AFB, a two-jet-engine transport with a capacity of about seven passengers (same as the North American Sabre Liner in civilian use).

High Flight—Stories of an Air Force Fighter Pilot

I married my wife, Carmella Coppola, in 1958 in New Jersey. She passed away in 1991. We have four children, Christopher, Leslie, Michele, and Colin. All of our kids were born in different locations, typical for a military family. My oldest son, Chris, was born while we were stationed at McGuire AFB in Mount Holly, New Jersey. My daughter, Leslie, was born in Washington, DC, while we were stationed in Louisiana and in the process of moving to England. My youngest children, Michele and Colin, were both born while we were stationed at Holloman AFB in Alamogordo, New Mexico. Military families bear a lot of the burden that we have to endure to serve our country.

I currently live in a military-sponsored retirement community near Fort Belvoir, Virginia, where many military heroes reside. In fact, meeting many of these retired heroes from all branches of the armed forces and hearing their amazing stories prompted me to write my own story.

I am grateful for my simple farm childhood in Rogersville, Alabama. Growing up in a large family, we relied on the land for our survival, but we also relied on the goodness of our neighbors and friends. When there was a tragedy, like our house fire or an economic downturn like the Depression, people in Rogersville were there for one another, our extended family. I will never forget the kindness of many neighbors and kin. Life on a farm was hard, but it gave me a strong moral compass and foundation for me to achieve my lofty goals as a career air force officer.

In our nation you can start your career on the bottom step of the ladder. As you move up, you have to adapt to those around you at the new level. You observe the most successful personnel around you and model their positive behavior. I believe that leadership is a combination of born talent and a learned behavior. It is no wonder that many in the world have a great desire to become citizens of our nation. As a cotton farmer's son, it has been truly a dream come true for me to be a part of the most capable air force in the world and to fly eight different jet fighters, some of them supersonic, during peacetime and in combat. A blessed and charmed life indeed, a high flight, soaring above the clouds where the view is unparalled and amazing.

Col. Lester Marlon Romine

Alaska Survival Training

High Flight—Stories of an Air Force Fighter Pilot

Captain Romine

Typical Bachelor officer quarters (BOQ

High Flight—Stories of an Air Force Fighter Pilot

Salmon Fishing in Alaska

Col. Lester Marlon Romine

Waterskiing in Florida during filming of the movie "Toward The Unknown"

Me and my wife Carmella 1958

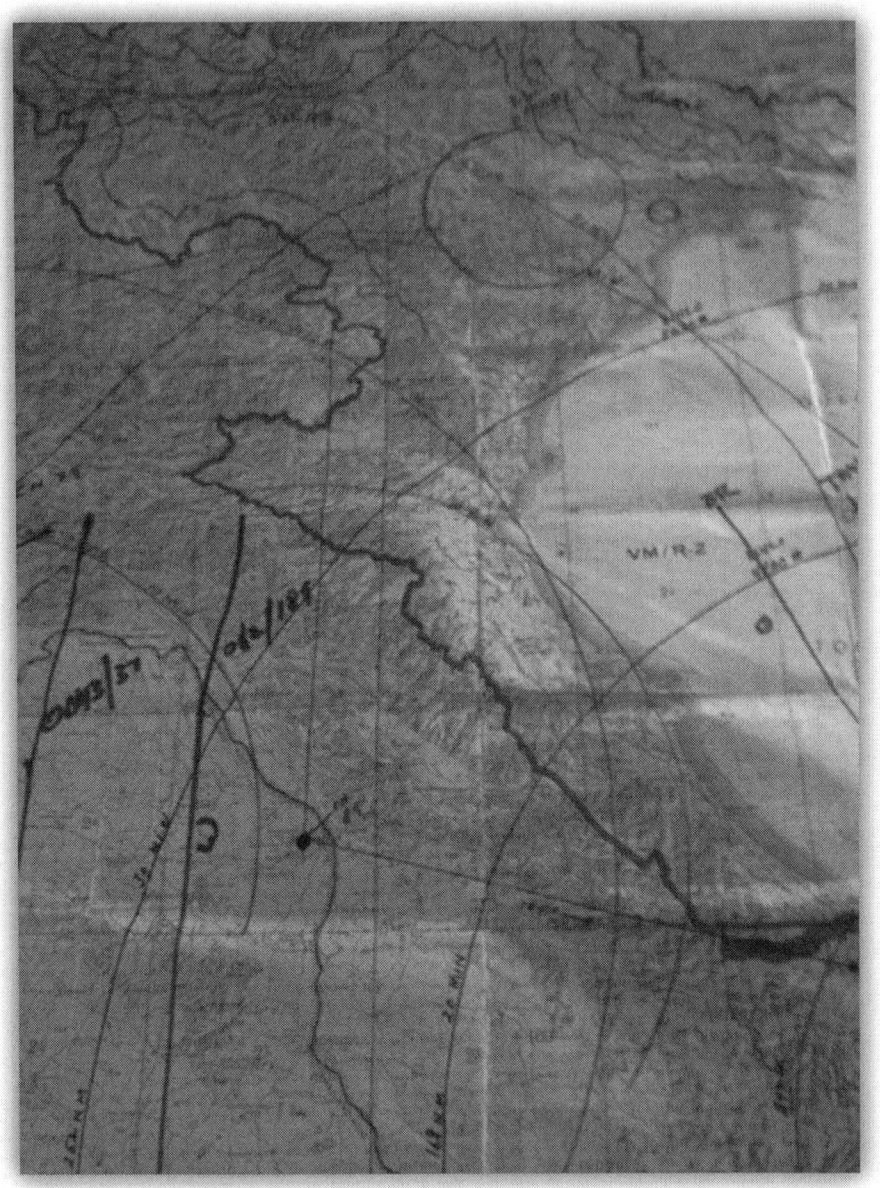

My map of Vietnam used during combat

From left to right: my niece Nicolette and my kids, Michele, Leslie, Christopher and Colin 1967

Medal Ceremony 1977 Langley AFB, Virginia

High Flight—Stories of an Air Force Fighter Pilot

Me and a few of my brothers 1972

Col. Lester Marlon Romine

Visiting my hometown 2005 with Michele and her kids

High Flight—Stories of an Air Force Fighter Pilot

Our farmhouse in Rogersville Alabama

My beloved mother, Katie Bedingfield Romine, on our farmhouse porch

High Flight—Stories of an Air Force Fighter Pilot

Me on the local transportation in Israel

About The Author

COLONEL LESTER ROMINE (USAF Retired) is the son of a cotton farmer who grew up in impoverished Depression-era Alabama. He went from picking cotton before school to Auburn University and enlisted in the US Air Force in 1950.

Romine's military career took him across the globe. He flew combat missions in Vietnam, sustaining his morale during the war with his strong Christian values and dedication to his country. Returning home, he continued his military career at the Pentagon, working in the field of computer automation. After twenty-seven years of service, he retired as a full colonel with many distinguished medals of honor.

Romine's coauthor is his daughter Michele Romine Treacy. A wife and mother, she holds a bachelor degree in mass communication and journalism from George Mason University. She is also a former television reporter.

Made in the USA
Middletown, DE
14 May 2018